THE POWER OF AND

THE POWER OF AND

Responsible Business Without Trade-Offs

R. EDWARD FREEMAN,
KIRSTEN E. MARTIN, AND
BIDHAN L. PARMAR

Columbia University Press

New York

Columbia University Press
Publishers Since 1893
New York   Chichester, West Sussex
cup.columbia.edu
Copyright © 2020 Columbia University Press
All rights reserved

Library of Congress Cataloging-in-Publication Data
Names: Freeman, R. Edward, 1951– author.
Title: The power of and : responsible business without trade-offs /
R. Edward Freeman, Kirsten E. Martin, and Bidhan L. Parmar.
Description: New York : Columbia University Press, [2020] |
Includes index.
Identifiers: LCCN 2019051351 (print) | LCCN 2019051352 (ebook) |
ISBN 9780231188500 (cloth) | ISBN 9780231547895 (ebook)
Subjects: LCSH: Social responsibility of business. |
Industries—Social aspects. | Entrepreneurship—Social aspects.
Classification: LCC HD60 .F722 2020 (print) |
LCC HD60 (ebook) | DDC 658.4/08—dc23
LC record available at https://lccn.loc.gov/2019051351
LC ebook record available at https://lccn.loc.gov/2019051352

Columbia University Press books are printed
on permanent and durable acid-free paper.

Printed in the United States of America

Cover design: Noah Arlow
Cover image: Getty Images

*To John Mackey, Kip Tindell, Tom and Dave Gardner,
Jeff Cherry, and all the other CEOs and executives who
are creating the new story of business with their companies.*

CONTENTS

ACKNOWLEDGMENTS

WE WISH to thank the following publishers and coauthors for granting us permission to rework some of the ideas contained in:

(1) "The Social Responsibility of Business Is to Create Value for Stakeholders." With H. Elms *MIT Sloan Management Review*, 2018; (2) "The New Story of Business: Towards a More Responsible Capitalism," *Business and Society Review*, 2017, 122:3, 449–465; (3) *Managing for Stakeholders*, with J. Harrison and A. Wicks (New Haven, CT: Yale University Press, 2007); and, (4) *Bridging the Values Gap*, with Ellen Auster (Oakland, CA: Berrett-Koehler, 2015).

In addition, we have benefited from critiques by students and colleagues from seminars at Bentley College, Bucknell University, University of Pittsburgh, Tampere University, The

Wharton School, Baruch College, Nottingham Trent University, HEC, Leuphana University, and numerous corporations and groups of executives from around the world.

We have also benefited greatly from a number of colleagues at universities around the world who have been working on the ideas in this book for many years. While there are so many working on "new story ideas," we want to especially mention Professors Ellen Auster and Robert Phillips (York University); Doug Bosse and Jeffrey Harrison (University of Richmond); Norman Bowie (University of Minnesota); Michel Dion (Sherbrooke University); Thomas Donaldson and Witold Henisz (Wharton, University of Pennsylvania); Elisabet Garriga (EADA); Jacob Hoerisch and Stefan Schalteger (Leuphana University); Johanna Kujala (Tampere University); Jeremy Moon and Metter Morsing (Copenhagen Business School); Mollie Painter (Nottingham Trent University); Sybille Sachs (HWZ); Raj Sisodia (Babson University); Rene Ten Bos (Radboud University); Bas Van der Linden (EDHEC); Chiara Vera (University of Torino); and many others.

Our colleagues and students at GWU and Darden have been a source of inspiration, particularly Greg Fairchild, Mary Margaret Frank, James Freeland, Yael Gruska-Cockayne, Elena Loutskina, Sankaran Venkataraman, Patricia Werhane, and Andrew Wicks.

Our debt to the Institute for Business in Society and the Olsson Center for Ethics at Darden is enormous. The tireless support from Executive Director Joey Burton and research and writing help from Sergiy Dmytriyev, Andrew Sell, Jenny Mead, and Karen Musselman have been instrumental in finishing the book.

ACKNOWLEDGMENTS

Myles Thompson, Brian Smith, and the team at Columbia University Press have been a joy to work with.

We are especially grateful to our families, who have put up with us during this process.

THE POWER OF AND

Chapter 1

THE NEW STORY OF BUSINESS

Key Ideas

- There is a growing conceptual revolution in how we think about business.
- The old narrative that business is only about the money is incomplete and no longer useful.
- There are many new, expansive models built on the five key ideas of (1) purpose; (2) stakeholder value; (3) business as a societal institution; (4) the complexity of people; and (5) the necessity to put business and ethics together.

THE SALESFORCE STORY

Salesforce is a remarkable software company that embodies and has helped define a new way to think about business.

Mark Benioff, the CEO, describes his view of business this way: "Companies can do more than just make money; they can serve others."[1] In a press release for Salesforce's *FY18 Stakeholder Impact Report*, Benioff provides his insights on the mission and purpose of business: "Truly great companies care about all of their stakeholders—employees, customers, partners, shareholders, the communities where we live and work, and the environment that sustains us. The business of business is to make the world a better place."[2] Benioff started Salesforce with the vision of making enterprise software easy to use and available over the internet. Salesforce built into its basic structure a model of giving back to society. Called "1-1-1," the model sets aside 1 percent of equity for community grants; donates 1 percent of the product to nonprofits and educational organizations; and donates 1 percent of employee time to communities.[3]

OVERALL ARGUMENT

Salesforce may seem like an outlier or an example that's too good to be true. But the basic ideas behind the Salesforce model are being replicated across the business landscape. From recent startups to long-standing companies, we are witnessing nothing less than a revolution in the way that we understand business. And according to Benioff, more and more business leaders are realizing that business can and indeed should seek to improve the state of the world.

What we expect from any business is in part determined by a very traditional story that emphasizes the need for companies to make profits for shareholders, the self-interested nature of human beings, and the separation of "business" from "ethics." In short, this traditional story focuses on the idea that business is just about the money. This story about our idea of "business" has long come under criticism, beginning a century ago with the debate between Harvard law professors Adolf A. Berle and E. Merrick Dodd.[4] It is not that the traditional story is wrong. Profits are important. Shareholders need to be satisfied. Markets are vital to business success. People can be self-interested. And sometimes it is difficult to reconcile business with ethics. However, when taken together, these assumptions make it difficult to improve business practice.

During one hundred years of debate to counter the anemic view that business is just about the money, many businesses have proposed a variety of alternative ideas, like "corporate social responsibility," "sustainability," "creating value for stakeholders," and "corporate stewardship."[5] And this debate has been carried out around the world. Indeed, there are very different systems of business that reflect different ideas about the central concepts and principles of business. In Germany, there is a system of joint governance between management and labor. In China, ownership by the state is widespread. In India, corporate social responsibility is a requirement. And in some Scandinavian countries, the idea of creating value for stakeholders is central.

We believe that almost all of these new, expansive "business models" revolve around five key ideas that need to be added to the traditional story of business: (1) the importance of purpose, values, and ethics, as well as profits; (2) the centrality of creating value for stakeholders, as well as shareholders; (3) seeing business as embedded both in societal institutions and in markets; (4) recognizing the full humanity of people, as well as their economic interests; and (5) integrating "business" and "ethics" into more holistic business models. When these ideas are combined, what emerges is a new story about the very nature of business, as well as a conception that is more aptly named "responsible business."

The plan of this book is as follows. In the remainder of this chapter, we will say more about why these new models have emerged and explore some of them in more detail. We will then explicate the five key ideas. In chapter 2, we will analyze what is wrong with the dominant idea of business and suggest that there are five questionable assumptions or myths about this old story. Chapters 3 through 7 each take one of the five new ideas and describe it in more detail, giving a wealth of examples of real companies that are using it to create value. Chapter 8 summarizes our argument and suggests some questions that companies can engage to begin to implement the new story of business.

THE FORCES THAT ARE BRINGING ABOUT THE NEW STORY OF BUSINESS

The global financial crisis (GFC) of 2008 has spawned an industry of analysis and calls for reform. While the forces that shaped the GFC had been emerging long before 2008, we see the GFC as a perfect storm that woke us up to the flaws in the way that we think about business. We believe that the GFC will be seen as a historical turning point in how we think about business and its role in society.

In addition to the GFC, globalization and the controversy surrounding it have a long history and a large impact on business. In the United States, globalization stems from the opening of trade in the post–World War II era. In many countries, globalization comes from the opening of borders to trade. More recently, technological forces such as the 24-7 news cycle, the internet, and companies like Google, Amazon, and Facebook have accelerated both globalization and reactions to it that embrace a new nationalism.

Alongside globalization, advances in information technology have increased our awareness of business's effects on the rest of society, solidifying the idea that business and ethics are, in fact, connected. We have most of the world's knowledge at our fingertips through Google and other search engines. Screens now mediate much of our human interaction. People use the internet to find relationships and life partners. And the existence of hacking, breaches of security, and the "dark web" implies that the old idea that "business ethics" is a contradiction needs to be replaced. It is difficult to explain these new businesses without also exploring ethical implications. One of the low points of the GFC was its devastating effects on communities. As credit became tighter around the world, many small businesses were forced to close. The variety of government responses reinforced the idea that business was not isolated in a so-called free market. Businesses realized that they were, in fact, embedded in society in a fundamental way. Of course, competitive economies and industries exist, but only in the context of societal institutions.

The arbitraging of tax payments across governments, economic and opportunity inequality, the specter of severe climate changes, and the effects of businesses on the communities where they operate have become important public policy issues around the world. And business has a role to play in all of them.

We have also seen changes in law and public policy in the United States and around the world. Many of these changes legitimize the idea that there must be limits on the goal of creating value for shareholders. In many states and countries, especially in Europe, corporate charters have evolved to prioritize creating value for stakeholders, not just shareholders.

Together these forces have encouraged entrepreneurs to think differently about the purpose of business. Many of these entrepreneurs focus on addressing societal problems that resulted from old ideas about capitalism. Many of these businesses were started because of concern with environmental issues, particularly climate change. And many traditional businesses, like Walmart and Unilever, have reorganized around understanding and mitigating their effects on the natural environment. Businesses that were built on the idea of "purpose greater than profits," such as The Container Store, have become a source of "new" models of business, even though many have a long history.

Even the Business Roundtable, an organization of about two hundred CEOs of the largest U.S. companies, has affirmed the idea that the old narrative of business is incomplete. Traditionally, the Roundtable had been firmly behind a "shareholder-centric" view of business. More recently, in August 2019, they issued a statement that said:[6]

While each of our individual companies serves its own corporate purpose, we share a fundamental commitment to all of our stakeholders. We commit to:

- Delivering value to our customers. We will further the tradition of American companies leading the way in meeting or exceeding customer expectations.
- Investing in our employees. This starts with compensating them fairly and providing important benefits. It also includes supporting them through training and education that help develop new skills for a rapidly changing world. We foster diversity and inclusion, dignity and respect.
- Dealing fairly and ethically with our suppliers. We are dedicated to serving as good partners to the other companies, large and small, that help us meet our missions.
- Supporting the communities in which we work. We respect the people in our communities and protect the environment by embracing sustainable practices across our businesses.
- Generating long-term value for shareholders, who provide the capital that allows companies to invest, grow, and innovate. We are committed to transparency and effective engagement with shareholders.
- Each of our stakeholders is essential. We commit to deliver value to all of them, for the future success of our companies, our communities, and our country.

While the statement has been met with skepticism in some quarters, we argue that it is a milestone in the conceptual revolution that is ongoing on many fronts, from entrepreneurs, Wall Street investors, and corporate leaders. The die has been cast, and there is no going back to the old story.

THE NEW MODELS

There are many proposals for business reform. Some of these models are relatively new, while others have a long history. Neither practitioners nor scholars are satisfied with the idea of business as primarily concerned with money and profits. Models for reform give rise to a better purpose and role for business in human society.

Perhaps the oldest model is **corporate social responsibility (CSR)**. The idea that business should contribute to society beyond its commercial operations has been circulating in the United States and around the world for centuries.[7] Corporate philanthropy, social giveback philosophies, community service, the executive as a public trustee, and other society-oriented ideas were quite well-known to American businesses and the public already in the 1920s. At that time, much of the thinking on corporate social responsibility came from influential business leaders themselves, who urged their companies to contribute to society beyond gaining profits.[8]

Corporate citizenship is the idea that business has to behave responsibly toward society, very much like a good citizen would do.[9] The link between corporate citizenship and CSR can also be seen in the world of business practitioners: many companies have introduced the language of good corporate citizenship into their CSR discourse.[10]

While thinking about how to take care of the environment may seem like a recent idea, the roots of the environmental movement are quite old. Nongovernmental organizations (NGOs) such as the Sierra Club were actually founded in the nineteenth-century conservation movement. The idea of **corporate sustainability** has spawned a number of new models of business. Its scope extends to nearly every aspect of corporate operations: economic sustainability, environmental sustainability, social sustainability, and ethical sustainability. Corporate sustainability suggests that a firm's business strategy should lie in the simultaneous, proactive pursuit of goals along all four of these dimensions. Managing a business according to the ideas of corporate sustainability will create sustainable long-term value for its stakeholders, which is a basis for a firm's sustainable development.

More recently, **stakeholder theory**[11] has become more widely accepted in business and academic circles, and it is foundational for responsible business. Stakeholder theory has challenged the pervasive idea that the primary responsibility of a company is a fiduciary duty to shareholders. It says that businesses should rather operate in the best interests of stakeholders, where shareholders are important but are only one group out of many. Stakeholders can be defined as "any group or individual who can affect or is affected by the achievement of organization's objectives," or as "any group or individual whose continued support is necessary for a company's existence and health." The Business

Roundtable enumerates key stakeholders as customers, suppliers, employees, communities, and shareholders.

Many new ideas about business build on the foundations of stakeholder theory, such as the model of **creating shared value (CSV)**.[12] CSV criticizes companies for ignoring society by focusing on optimizing short-term financial performance. Nestlé has been a leader in pioneering the CSV model, especially in its supply-chain relationships.

John Mackey and Raj Sisodia have proposed a new model called **conscious capitalism**. This model is based on a number of companies, including Whole Foods Market, which was cofounded by Mackey. The basic idea is that businesses have to operate with a much higher level of consciousness about their overall purpose and their impact on the world around them. Conscious capitalism is grounded in four major pillars: higher purpose, stakeholder integration, conscious leadership, and conscious culture. These pillars are interrelated, and each of them is essential to building an economic system that embraces human dignity and freedom.[13]

Inclusive capitalism is yet another example of a concept that emerged out of the growing criticism of capitalism as an economic system that failed to provide prosperous well-being for a large part of society. Some business and government leaders, as well as scholars and social activists, became concerned with the mounting income inequality and a significant drop of public trust in business after the financial crisis of 2008. They saw a pressing need for business to intentionally make efforts to alleviate poverty by serving previously underserved segments of the market.[14]

The B Corp movement, created in 2006, is another example. Practitioners founded the movement to propagate the stakeholder theory that a company's purpose and stakeholders do matter. Inspired by the idea that taking care of stakeholders is essential for any business, B Corps consider the impact of their decisions on their workers, customers, suppliers, community, and the environment. Companies are welcome to join the movement if they agree to operate according to the B Corp declaration, which requires that businesses be "purpose-driven and create . . . benefit for all stakeholders, not just shareholders."[15]

Many individual business practitioners, including high-profile business leaders, are eager to improve the way capitalism functions. The British billionaire Richard Branson came up with **Capitalism 24902**, named after the planet Earth's 24,902-mile circumference. The main idea is that business needs "to stop the downward spiral we all find ourselves in" by taking care of both the people and the planet that together make up our global village.[16]

Inspired by the same idea to make capitalism better, former chairman and CEO of the Coca-Cola Company, Neville Isdell, coined the term **connected capitalism**, which stands for connecting firms' bottom lines to a social conscience. Criticizing the corporate greed and mismanagement that permeate the contemporary business landscape, connected capitalism urges companies to make a positive change in the world. To tackle social issues, it is not enough just to create nonprofits because the scale of many societal problems requires the involvement of business. That is why many high-profile executives in major companies including Coca-Cola, UPS, and SunTrust Banks have signed up for the ideas of connected capitalism.[17]

Social entrepreneurship emphasizes the role of business in contributing to solving social and environmental issues. Unlike stakeholder theory or CSR, which aims to change established business practices throughout the entire business arena, social entrepreneurship primarily targets start-up companies and entrepreneurs. Social entrepreneurship focuses on creating new ventures that, from the very first day of their existence, would target poverty alleviation, environmental protection, or community development.

THE WALL STREET RESPONSE

Initially, investors on Wall Street were extremely skeptical of this mixing of business and societal issues, no matter how it was done. There was a long history of **socially responsible investing**,[18] in which investors use predetermined criteria to screen out so-called sin companies, whose profits come from tobacco, alcohol, defense, etc. While those socially responsible funds are still in operation, the concern with the issues we have outlined has greatly surpassed these investment screens. By some estimates, over $30 trillion is under management that ascribes to one or more of these new business models.[19] Today, a number of new investment models are sweeping Wall Street. Here are a few of the salient ones.

Impact investing characterizes investments that are intentionally made to address social and environmental issues.

Impact investors reject the narrow-minded view that the single objective of any business investment is to gain lucrative financial returns. Similarly, impact investment is based on the premise that social and environmental impacts can be achieved alongside profitable economic activity. Impact investing has found support from the Catholic Church, which sees potential in the idea of investing money and doing good at the same time. Impact investing works best in a close collaboration among different stakeholders, such as government and nonprofit institutions, "with each part playing a more powerful role because of its complementarity."[20]

Some experts have argued that society needs capitalists who can start and run legal companies.[21] We need many more Bill Gateses and fewer foundations. People grow out of poverty when they create small businesses that employ their neighbors. The solution is **patient capital**. Patient capital, also called long-term investment, has gained popularity in the era of increased corporate responsibility. People realize that "we need both the market and we need aid . . . patient capital works between, and tries to take the best of both."[22] Patient capital does not require immediate returns but instead looks at business profitability from a long-term perspective. It believes in investing in local entrepreneurs who know what problems their communities face and are ready to experiment with finding effective solutions. Patient capital is especially relevant in the light of an increasingly popular phenomenon nowadays—social entrepreneurship.[23]

One of the catchall titles for these new models of investment on Wall Street is **ESG** (environment, society, and governance). ESG is often used to refer to any of these specific investment screens, or indeed any investment screen that takes societal factors into account. Many investment firms have signed onto the United Nations's Principles of Responsible Investing, which incorporates ESG issues:[24]

As institutional investors, we have a duty to act in the best long-term interests of our beneficiaries. In this fiduciary role, we believe that environmental, social, and corporate governance (ESG) issues can affect the performance of investment portfolios (to varying degrees across companies, sectors, regions, asset classes and through time). We also recognize that applying these Principles may better align investors with broader objectives of society.

The six principles then outline the importance of ESG ideas and that of full disclosure around the principles. Signatories to the principles have over $70 trillion under management. No longer is Wall Street lagging behind the emergence of this new narrative about business.

MEASURING BUSINESS AND SOCIETAL IMPACT

One of the critiques of these new models and Wall Street's interest in them is that there is not yet any agreement on how to measure results. The idea that profit measured the total performance of a business was a key piece of the old story. But there are many measurements, beyond just profit, that can be made and tailored to the situation of a particular business. A number of newly developed models explicitly try to address this measurement issue: JUST Capital, triple bottom line, integrated reporting, the Global Reporting Initiative, and the Sustainable Development Goals.

JUST Capital is among the most recent concepts whose ideas support the new story of business. Introduced in 2013, JUST Capital, like many other concepts discussed above, argues that the world needs fair and equal treatment for all employees; strong, prosperous communities; and a healthy planet—and these goals can be achieved by public companies. Following their belief that, in capitalism, business should constantly strive to make positive changes in the world, the founders of the JUST Capital movement created a ranking of just companies so that potential customers, employees, and investors can make informed decisions on what products to buy, whom to work for, or where to invest.[25]

Triple bottom line (3BL) is an accounting methodology that aims to evaluate a company's performance holistically. Unlike a traditional accounting framework, which measures only the economic bottom line, 3BL also accounts for a company's social performance and ecological impact.[26]

Integrated reporting has been established to develop accountability, stewardship, and trust by restructuring information flow coming from business. It was created to tie together financial stability and sustainable development by making corporate reporting more transparent and inclusive, and also less complex. In 2010, the Prince of Wales initiated a meeting among business representatives from different areas—companies, investors, accountants, standard developers, as well as UN legislatures—to create the International Integrated Reporting Committee (IIRC) to coordinate the implementation of integrated reporting across the globe. As of 2019, about two thousand organizations are using integrated reporting.

The Global Reporting Initiative (GRI) was developed in collaboration with the UN Environment Programme. Headquartered in Amsterdam, GRI helps companies evaluate and report their impact on environmental, social, and economic areas by applying its sustainability reporting standards "developed with true multi-stakeholder contributions and rooted in the public interest." As of May 2019, there were over six hundred companies worldwide using the GRI reporting guidelines, including Abbott, Bayer AG, Dell, Honda, Nike, PwC, Coca-Cola, and UPS.[27]

Growing signs of the new story of business are seen not only in business but everywhere with the development of the **Sustainable Development Goals** (SDG). In 2015, more than 190 countries of the United Nations General Assembly adopted the 2030 Agenda for Sustainable Development, which includes seventeen main goals: no poverty; zero hunger; good health and well-being; quality education; gender equality; clean water and sanitation; affordable and clean energy; decent work and economic growth; industry, innovation, and infrastructure; reduced inequalities; sustainable cities and communities; responsible consumption and production; climate action; life below water; life on land; peace, justice and strong institutions; and partnerships for the goals. To make sure that countries deliver on the defined goals, a list of 169 tangible targets was developed, with each target holding from one to three indicators to measure whether organizations are making progress. With the launch of an open-access tracker in 2018, it became easy to track the progress toward SDG across the globe.[28]

KEY IDEAS BEHIND THE NEW MODELS

At two 2016 meetings at the White House sponsored by the Obama Administration's Department of Labor, seventy-five people from a variety of organizations and movements gathered to discuss whether or not there needed to be one brand that identifies the emerging new story of business. While such a brand may someday surface, for our purposes we want to focus on the underlying ideas and principles that are inspiring all of this activity. Whatever brand ultimately becomes the rallying cry of this conceptual revolution, it will have to be based on a sense of purpose and ethics that is as central to the new narrative as profit is to the old one. It will have to address how companies can simultaneously create value for all of their key stakeholders. The brand will have to take sustainability and the physical limits of business very seriously. It will have to account for the fact that all businesses are embedded in societal institutions and processes. It will have to recognize that people are complex and that they can and do collaborate with others to create value. And it will have to integrate these ideas into a coherent framework. Let's explain each of these ideas and show how they work together.

To summarize, the five key ideas that undergird the new story of responsible business are as follows: (1) Purpose, values, and ethics are as important as money/profits. (2) Business is about value creation for stakeholders. (3) Business is embedded in society and in a physical world. (4) People are complex. (5) Business and ethics must be integrated into holistic business models. Let's briefly look at each in turn and see how they are connected.

PURPOSE, VALUES, AND ETHICS ARE AS IMPORTANT AS MONEY/PROFITS

One of the great things about business as an institution is that many different purposes are possible. Novo Nordisk wants to rid the world of diabetes. Whole Foods Market wants to help people be healthier with better food choices. Tastings, a small restaurant in Charlottesville, Virginia, wants to bring the joy of good French country cooking to its customers. The founders of Relish MBA want to make it easier for companies and MBA students to find a good match. The only limit to the purpose of a business is our imagination. Of course, purposes aren't necessarily good. We have plenty of examples from human history about organizations whose purpose was morally evil. A sense of values and ethics has to go alongside purpose. Many organizations that ascribe to the new story of responsible business are addressing precisely this issue. Almost every one of the new models mentioned above have a place in them for the idea of purpose. We can no longer make the mistake that the pursuit of profits is the sole purpose of business. Real purpose inspires employees as well as other stakeholders who come to share that purpose. Purpose makes this new story of business an inspirational one.

At Salesforce, purpose and values are front and center throughout the company. They are both top-down and bottom-up. Every employee is trained (and gets certified) on the company's purpose and values, and there are constant conversations about them throughout the company. In fact, Salesforce has invented a management process, called "V2MOM" (vision, values, methods, obstacles, and measures), to keep these conversations alive even in the face of Salesforce's remarkable growth rate. Marc Benioff describes the process as follows:[29]

> V2MOM enabled me to clarify what I was doing and communicate it to the entire company as well. The vision helped us define what we wanted to do. The values established what was most important about that vision; it set the principles and beliefs that guided it (in priority). The methods illustrated how we would get the job done by outlining the actions and the steps that everyone needed to take. The obstacles identified the challenges, problems, and issues we would have to overcome to achieve our vision. Finally, the measures specified the actual result we aimed to achieve; often this was defined as a numerical outcome. Combined, V2MOM gave us a detailed map of where we were going as well as a compass to direct us there.

Organizations like Salesforce, Tastings, Whole Foods, and Novo Nordisk focus on both purpose and profits.

BUSINESS IS ABOUT VALUE CREATION FOR STAKEHOLDERS

One of the cornerstones of the new story of business is looking beyond shareholders to a broader group of stakeholders. From older models like CSR to newer ones like JUST Capital ratings, creating value for stakeholders is one of the most important ideas in the new story. It is something that every successful business has actually done. As business people become more aware of this fact, they can build more nuanced ways of creating value into their business models.

It has often been said that the key insight of stakeholder theory is that shareholders are not the only group that is important. Another insight is even more important: stakeholder interests are interdependent. When management can capture this interdependence and push it forward, great results are likely to occur. For many years, Walmart was a poster child for this interdependence. By negotiating tough deals with suppliers, Walmart could offer customers low prices. Even though the margins were thin for suppliers, the huge volume could lead to profitability. Employees were better off because there were more customers coming to take advantage of the low prices, which meant more opportunities for employees. The stock price saw a steady increase. Unfortunately, Walmart paid little attention to communities as stakeholders. Many outside groups formed in protest, and Walmart was blamed for many social ills. Today, Walmart is working hard to repair its relationships with communities and to integrate ideas that improve communities into its business model. The progress it has made with sustainability is one of several examples where Walmart has taken a leadership role.

Salesforce's overall philosophy is that great companies must serve stakeholders, not just shareholders. Salesforce employees try to take the perspective of stakeholders. They spend a lot of time engaged with stakeholders, attending and sponsoring hundreds of conferences with customers and suppliers and other partners. Special events like Dreamforce (an annual conference) and Trailhead (a program of online tutorials to teach coding skills) engage with stakeholders. Salesforce has created an entire ecosystem with their stakeholders and partners. The company uses its own software to stay in touch, to train, and to retrain; they estimate that this partner ecosystem will create more than three million jobs by 2022.[30]

BUSINESS IS EMBEDDED IN SOCIETY AND IN A PHYSICAL WORLD

Business is not an isolated institution that stands alone in some kind of moral free zone. It is firmly embedded in other social institutions, such as governments, families, religious institutions, etc. And it is firmly grounded in the real, physical world. While many who write about sustainability and the environment sound a cautionary note about the physical limits of the world, this is only part of the story. We need to come to see business as embodied in the world and recognize that the physical world imposes constraints. We also need to see business as capable of transforming those constraints into new opportunities. We have seen this time and again as companies such as 3M figure out how to turn waste streams into products and services. Obviously we need to tackle climate change, but to see climate change as limiting growth is to forget the creative imagination that has solved so many of our problems in the past. Adopting some kind of green values, as well as integrating respect for the environment into our purpose and values, can be a powerful elixir for creativity.[31]

At Salesforce, the volunteer effort that starts on the day that an employee is hired goes a long way in creating connections between Salesforce and the rest of society. By building philanthropy into its basic business model, Salesforce connects to its stakeholders and its communities from the very start. It has created a platform for change in communities, especially around education, giving over $50 million in donations to public schools. It also sees the environment as a key stakeholder. Salesforce has achieved net-zero greenhouse gas emissions and a carbon-neutral cloud service. And the company is working to integrate sustainability into all of its operations, as well as leveraging its employees to work towards a more sustainable world.[32]

PEOPLE ARE COMPLEX

Part of the old narrative of business is that most people are self-interested and need incentives to really work in business. However, a much more inspirational view of human beings has emerged. People are using business models and ideas to attack age-old problems of poverty, education, disease, and lack of participation in society. Often these problems are addressed by these "new story companies" in conjunction with NGOs, governments, and other private organizations. We have seen a wave of "social entrepreneurs" and "impact investing," where the explicit idea is to use business to make society better and to solve social problems. We are fast crafting a new idea about what it is to be human. Business is embedded in society and is often run by people who have multiple goals and identities, people who are not just "rent-seekers" looking to manipulate resources or policies for economic gain without giving back to society.

What is a smartphone, really? The way we see it, it's some bits of sand and metal, some vocabularies that we have invented to solve problems, and the fact that we can work together collaboratively to achieve things that no one of us can achieve alone. In short, we see the world not as a world of scarcity, but as one of abundance. We have an almost infinite capacity to invent ways to solve our problems, whether we take on poverty, space travel, climate change, or understanding the rules of cricket. We are not in it alone. We invent mutually beneficial vocabularies with others to solve our problems. This is true whether we are scientists or politicians. We are surely more than narrow economic creatures. Capitalism works because of this complex human dimension.

Salesforce encourages its people to bring their whole selves to work recognizing the richness that is present in the full humanity of its employees. The company has also invented systems for people to support each other, air grievances, and form working groups around a number of issues important to employees. Recently, Salesforce conducted an audit around equal pay; given the results of the audit, they adjusted salaries for men and women to ensure equal pay.[33]

BUSINESS AND ETHICS MUST BE INTEGRATED INTO HOLISTIC BUSINESS MODELS

One way to summarize these ideas is to say that business and ethics must go together. We have to integrate our economic interests with our broader human interests, and our models of business need to reflect this integration. We can no longer afford an idea of business that is narrowly economic, in terms of focusing on profits and money, either leaving the rest of our interests to government or pretending that markets will eventually work things out for the best. Many of the worst outcomes occur because of narratives about business that separate business decisions from ethical decisions. This is seen most clearly in the popular joke about *business ethics* being an oxymoron. In reality, almost any business decision has some ethical content. To see that this is true we need only ask whether the following questions make sense for virtually any business decision:

- Who is harmed by and/or who benefits from this decision?
- Whose rights are enabled and whose values are realized by this decision, and whose are not?
- What kind of person will I (we) become if I (we) make this decision?
- What relationships will be strengthened or weakened by this decision?

Since these questions are present in every business decision, although they might not be top of mind for a specific decision maker, it is reasonable to see ethics as an integral part of business. Even Milton Friedman argues that companies should make a profit "while conforming to the basic rules of the society, both those embodied in law and those embodied in ethical custom."[34] Ethics is about the principles, consequences, matters of character, and relationships that we use to live together.

At Salesforce, conversations around ethics and values are everyday occurrences. Recently, the company opened an office of ethics and humane use, recognizing that their own technologies open up ethics questions with no ready answers.[35] Recently, the company took a stand on gun control. They asked their customers to either stop selling semiautomatic rifles or stop using Salesforce's software.[36]

Unless we want to repeat the problems of the old story of business, each of the new models must address how business and ethics are connected. Doing so generates trust, and it sets expectations that most people will generally keep their promises and take responsibility for their actions. If this is not the case, then, as Adam Smith told us, markets and organizations just won't work very well. To create value, it is more effective to focus on integrating business and ethics within a complex set of stakeholder relationships, rather than treating ethics as a side constraint on making profits.

■ ■ ■

These five ideas are mutually supportive of each other. Because purpose matters, those people and groups who are affected by a purpose must be engaged. Stakeholders are themselves engaged with the creation of value for others. And we are all embedded in our societal institutions in a network of complex human relationships. Successful businesses and other organizations figure out how to put these ideas together into a business model that integrates economic, financial, social, political, and moral issues in a way that garners stakeholder support and realizes the purpose of the organization.

No company is perfect, nor can any company become perfect. For many of the companies we have already mentioned, some critics will respond that they have failed to live up to their professed values in one or another circumstance. This criticism is often correct. What is problematic is that many critics divide businesses into "saints" and "sinners." Sinners are driven by profits and money, and saints have a noble and altruistic intent. If our argument is correct, there are very few sinners and even fewer saints. Oscar Wilde perhaps put it best: every saint has a past, and every sinner has a future.

"Saints and sinners" thinking gets us into trouble. We begin by assuming most businesses are sinners and then scrutinizing those few who we think might be saints. Saints-and-sinners thinking breeds skepticism about any action that is not clearly a profit-maximizing one. The new story of business is a more optimistic and hopeful one. Yes, companies do bad things, sometimes intentionally and sometimes mistakenly. Sometimes the world changes and old business models are no longer appropriate. However, the new story asks us to hold off on immediate skepticism. It suggests that we should come to expect our businesses to make our societies and communities better. That is in fact what is happening in businesses all around the world. We need to loosen the grip of saints-and-sinners thinking and see our ability to cooperate together, invent solutions to our problems, and create value for each other as central to the human experience. We need to more carefully understand just what is wrong with the old narrative of business.

Chapter 2

WHAT'S WRONG WITH THE TRADITIONAL STORY OF BUSINESS

Key Ideas

- The idea that business exists only to make money is incomplete logically, empirically, and practically.
- Shareholders are not the owners of large public companies, nor do they deserve managers' full attention.
- The traditional story of business is incomplete and provides only part of the story of how business works.
- Business does not exist in a vacuum.
- Business and ethics can't be separated.

AN ENDLESS CYCLE OF SCANDAL AND BAD NEWS: THE TRADITIONAL NARRATIVE

Think about the following company names:

- Enron
- Volkswagen
- Worldcom
- Wells Fargo
- Parmalat
- Purdue Pharma
- Uber
- Facebook
- Samsung

What do these corporate icons have in common? Unfortunately, they have all been implicated in some kind of scandal in the recent past. And these names don't include the companies that went bankrupt or almost bankrupt because they were obsessed with shareholder value, understood in very narrow terms. They were in the grip of a traditional idea about business that is deep within our culture, and it is an idea that we should abandon.

The current version of this traditional story of business is best summarized by a famous 1970 *New York Times Magazine* article in which Chicago economist Milton Friedman declared that the only legitimate goal for executives was to maximize profits for shareholders.[1] This quickly became a mantra for thinking about business. Only a few years later, two finance professors,

Michael Jensen and William Meckling, declared that share-holder value should be the sole objective of companies in order to create the most wealth possible.[2]

In the nearly fifty years since Friedman's original article, there have been many pages written criticizing or defending the view that making profits for shareholders is the sole legitimate objective of business. The debate has ranged across disciplines from law to corporate finance and economics to ethics to polit-ical science and others. There are a number of versions of this dominant narrative. We have identified five key ideas common to the debate: (1) the sole purpose of business is to make profits; (2) business is primarily about serving shareholders, the legiti-mate "owners" of the business; (3) business works best when it is allowed to operate in free and unregulated markets; (4) busi-nesspeople are purely economic creatures; and (5) business and ethics should be separated.

There are a number of ways to state these assumptions. They can be stated as matters of fact, for example, people simply are always self-interested, and they in fact always do act in their economic self-interest. Or, the assumptions can be put in more normative terms—such as, for business to work best, business-people should act in their economic self-interest. Or they can be explained in a mixture of these two modes—such as most people, most of the time, act in their self-interest, and business thrives because of it. Some business thinkers believe that only the factual approach has merit, but others recognize that this dominant narrative about business is itself a matter of values and ethics—it's a choice that we make that shapes our behavior. In either case, we believe that these assumptions aren't very useful for understanding business in the twenty-first century. They tell only part of the real story. Let's consider these ideas one by one. We are going to call them "myths about business."

MYTH #1: THE SOLE PURPOSE OF BUSINESS IS TO MAKE PROFITS[3]

During the global financial crisis, many banks were leveraged at a rate of 30 to 1 with synthetic collateralized debt obligations (CDOs). Michael Lewis's book, *The Big Short*, details how the dogged pursuit of shareholder value caused layoffs, bankruptcy, bad customer relationships, and a number of other painful and unpleasant outcomes.

Our experience with friends, MBA students, the media, and many others is that there is a dominant belief that business is primarily "about the money." This belief has a number of forms. One way to state it is that business is—or should be—primarily about making money and profits for shareholders. Business is, in this view, "the physics of money," and the language of money and profits is seen by many as the main metaphor when we talk about business. Watch any business-oriented news network, and you will find almost an obsession with earnings, profits, share prices, and factors that will affect them. Often these pundits (as well as the theorists they rely on) talk as if money is the only thing that matters, and the vocabulary of finance and accounting are the only vocabularies used to tell us how to build a great business. More precisely, business is seen as a collection of economic transactions that can be fully understood using economic models and concepts. Modern economics has built powerful models, from general equilibrium theory to modern econometrics, and indeed they are useful for understanding how markets work. The problem is that these models are not the only way to understand business, and they can be misleading, as the global financial crisis (GFC) taught us.

We believe this idea that the only purpose of business is to make profits rests on a simple logic mistake. First of all, we have to recognize that every business needs money to operate, and over the long term, every business must be profitable, or it will die. Profits (or free cash flow, to be more precise) are a necessary condition for a successful business to continue to operate. We often see in the popular press a discounting of the very idea of profits, and even that profits themselves are somehow evil. Such an idea is foolishness, as every business needs to earn an excess over paying its bills in order to invest in the future. But it doesn't follow from this fact about the necessity of profits that the sole purpose of business is to make profits. In fact, it doesn't follow that the purpose of a business is in any way connected to the need to make money if it is to survive.

An analogy is helpful here. We need red blood cells to live. Making red blood cells is a necessary process to remain among the living. However, the purpose of life is not to simply make red blood cells. Purpose is something else. It is a *raison d'être*, a reason for being. Purpose inspires us. It offers us a reason for our actions. It motivates us to cooperate with others to bring great ideas to life.

Most entrepreneurs don't start a business because they are only interested in the money. Most of them have an idea that they want to share with the world, that they are "on fire" about, whether it's the personal computer revolution, like Steve Jobs and Bill Gates, or helping people eat in a healthier way, like John Mackey of Whole Foods Market.

Of course, there is an element of truth in this focus on money because it is necessary to make money in order to sustain a business. (Note that this is true of all organizations. There must be some way to sustain "paying the bills.") To return to our analogy, sometimes people have to focus on making red blood cells, say after a surgery or an injury where there has been blood loss. However, it still doesn't follow that making red blood cells is the purpose of life. In the real business world, sometimes things go awry and a business needs to focus on the short term, righting the ship, and making enough money to continue to exist. A competitor can disrupt an industry, or executives may have made a mistake, or the world may simply have changed. In all of these cases, a business might have to focus on generating profits to simply stay alive, but it would be a mistake to claim that making profits is its sole purpose.

MYTH #2: BUSINESS IS ABOUT SERVING SHAREHOLDERS AND FINANCIERS

According to the former CEO of Valeant Pharmaceuticals, "All I care about is shareholders." When Valeant slashed R&D costs and initiated a strategy of buying companies through debt financing and raising drug prices, it came under investigation for fraud, price gouging, and other criminal charges. Ironically, these moves, which were intended to create shareholder value, backfired and ended up destroying a great deal of shareholder value.[4]

Connected to the idea that business is ultimately about the money is the notion that profits are for shareholders and maybe other financiers such as banks and bondholders. The dominant story tells us that shareholders own the business and that managers and executives "work for" the shareholders. While this too-convenient fiction may be true in some jurisdictions around the world, in the United States it is debatable, if not false. Indeed, former General Electric CEO Jack Welch has called the idea of maximizing shareholder value "the dumbest idea in the world."[5]

Some have argued that shareholders do not own companies. According to U.S. law, public companies own themselves and are their own legal entities. Corporations are distinct entities that own property but are not property themselves. Shareholders own shares, which involves a contract with this legally independent entity.[6] Depending on the nature of the contract, the shareholder has specific rights and responsibilities. Some shares carry voting rights, and owning a majority of those shares can allow a particular individual or institutional investor to control seats on the board and to influence company management. Other classes of shares do not have voting rights. Many companies have multiple classes of shares with different voting rights. In 2017, SNAP was the first initial public offering (IPO) in U.S. history to not offer any voting shares to the public.[7] Public companies, shareholders, and shares are too diverse to be accurately reflected in the simple statement, "Shareholders own companies."

Moreover, it is far too simple to say that managers "work for shareholders." Directors have a "duty of care," a legal obligation (in the United States) to do what is best for the corporation. Of course, this includes shareholders, but it can encompass duties to other stakeholders as well. Students in finance are sometimes taught that managers are the agents of shareholders, who are the principals. However, according to U.S. law, shareholders are not principals, and managers are not their agents. In 1976, Jensen and William Meckling,[8] the finance theorists who created the principal/agent model, borrowed legal terminology from the law of agency that originally developed in England to determine the question of whether a lord or master was responsible for the actions of its serfs or slaves.

Sometimes students believe that if executives and directors don't maximize shareholder value, they will be sued or fired. That may be the case in some corporations where certain shareholders have a controlling interest, but in most cases the courts rely on what they call the "business judgment rule." Professor Lynn Stout argues that the rule states that as long as "a board of directors is not tainted by personal conflicts of interest and makes a reasonable effort to become informed, courts will not second guess the board's decisions about what is best for the company—even when those are decisions that seem to harm shareholder value."[9] For example, the company that owned the Chicago Cubs baseball team refused to hold night games because it took the position that baseball should be a daytime sport. Holding night games would have increased profits. When the company was sued, the court ruled that under the business judgment rule, it could not disturb the board's decision, absent any evidence of fraud, illegality, or conflict of interest.[10] As evidenced by the court ruling, the business judgment rule allows a wide range of autonomy for executives. As long as they don't put profits in their own pockets, they can spend on employees, pursue low-profit projects, or buy corporate jets—no matter what the effect on shareholder value.

In contrast to the absence of special obligations to shareholders, the law actually requires that corporations take into consideration the claims of customers, suppliers, local communities, and employees. For example, the U.S. Consumer Product Safety Commission has the power to enact product recalls, essentially leading to an increase in the number of voluntary product recalls by companies seeking to mitigate legal damage awards. Thus companies must take the interests of customers into account by law. The National Labor Relations Act gave employees the right to unionize and bargain in good faith. It set up the National Labor Relations Board to enforce these rights with management. The Equal Pay Act of 1963 and Title VII of the Civil Rights Act of 1964 constrain management from discrimination in hiring practices; these rules have aligned corporate practice with employee rights. Similarly, the law has also evolved to try to protect the interests of local communities. The Clean Air Act and the Clean Water Act, as well as various amendments to these classic pieces of legislation, have constrained management from "spoiling the commons." Even shareholders get into the act with protections enacted by the Securities and Exchange Commission to keep the idea of fair markets.

The main idea behind focusing on shareholder value was to make companies more efficient and profitable. Now, given more than forty years of evidence, we can see whether this strategy has worked. A recent analysis by the consulting firm Deloitte suggests that return on invested capital in the United States has steadily decreased since 1965, from an average of 4.2 percent to 1.2 percent in 2009.[11] There is no clear evidence that firms aiming to maximize shareholder value actually perform better than other companies. There is some evidence that they perform worse. The irony is that shareholders can also be made worse off when executives try to maximize shareholder value.

Public companies are also disappearing as more firms choose to stay private and merge with other companies to provide economies of scale. In 1995, there were 7,322 U.S. public companies; today, that number is less than 3,700.[12] Public companies are not living as long; in 1958, the average lifespan of a U.S. public company was 61 years, in 1980, it was 25 years, and in 2015, it had fallen to 10 years.[13] Additionally, short-termism is growing faster as shareholders demand more immediate results. In 1960, the average shareholder held a stock for about eight years; in 2010, that number was down to four months.

Of course, as with all the parts of the dominant story, there is an element of truth here. Shareholders and other financiers are important. Indeed, they are stakeholders too. Framing an argument as "shareholders versus stakeholders" is unproductive. And sometimes executives need to focus on shareholders, just as there are times when they need to focus on customers. However, over a corporation's lifespan, all stakeholder interests have to be kept in balance or harmony, so focusing on either shareholders or employees exclusively is likely to lead to poor performance.

MYTH #3: BUSINESS IS BEST UNDERSTOOD AS FREE AND UNREGULATED MARKETS

Hailed as the one of the most innovative companies, Enron became embroiled in one of the signature scandals of the twenty-first century. Investigators found that Enron's attempts to fool regulators with fake holdings and off-the-books accounting were a large part of its collapse.[14]

A key part of the dominant narrative about business is that business as a system can best thrive in "free markets." While the exact nature of "free markets" is often left undetermined, many believe the term refers to a largely unregulated market, free of government interference and regulation: the market itself will sort out winners and losers. Perhaps the biggest proponent of this view was the novelist Ayn Rand, whose 1957 novel *Atlas Shrugged* is still the favorite of many U.S. CEOs. Rand believed that if businesses relied on government assistance, then the resulting companies would be dependent on it. The ensuing economy, based on "crony capitalism," would discourage the creative genius of the heroic entrepreneur.

While Rand and others are undoubtedly correct about the desirability of a system free of crony capitalism, any viable idea of "free markets" must stop short of a system of anything goes. Business is set within a societal framework, connected with its communities. Employees live in towns and cities and need roads, schools, and health care if they are to thrive. Customers need to be able to redress wrongs that inevitably emerge as companies make mistakes or even harm them intentionally. Indeed, as we saw in the previous section, laws emerged so customers, suppliers, employees, communities, and financiers have some measure of protection.

Perhaps the most crucial issue of our day is what to do about climate change and global warming. Here, no single company and no single government can solve the issue alone. Action needs to be coordinated across institutions. Indeed, many multi-stakeholder partnerships are emerging to tackle this complex of issue. The idea that multi-stakeholder partnerships are somehow opposed to the idea of a free market is a function of the old narrative.

One important assumption of the old narrative that rings true is that the most effective action is likely to be voluntary. Responsible business works because it is built on the creativity and voluntary actions of many individuals and companies. The "free" in "free markets" is crucial, whether or not we understand "markets" in their purely economic sense or not.

MYTH #4: BUSINESS PEOPLE ARE PURELY ECONOMIC CREATURES

Uber was severely criticized for "price gouging" when it applied its surge pricing methodology during a 2017 terrorist attack in New York City and earlier in 2014 during a hostage crisis in Sydney. While surge pricing is based on the simple economics of supply and demand, the criticism has given Uber food for thought about when to apply the method. Shortly after the New York City attack, Uber suspended surge pricing.[15]

The dogma that most people act only in their economic self-interest is perhaps the most damaging part of the old narrative. This unidimensional view of human behavior has a long history of being incorrect. Anyone who has ever been in love or who has parented a child knows that self-interest has limited explanatory power.

However, there is a grain of truth to the idea that we act in our own self-interest. First of all, we act in our own narrow, short-term self-interest, although it may not be in our longer-term interest. This is especially true of people who suffer from psychological syndromes such as narcissism, putting themselves and their own interests front and center in all situations. Second, "self-interest" can have a broader definition. For instance, acting in the interests of our loved ones or family members or others we are connected to is acting in our self-interest. Acting in a way that helps others can also be in our self-interest, at least according to Adam Smith. He famously says:[16] "How selfish soever man may be supposed, there are evidently some principles in his nature, which interest him in the fortune of others, and render their happiness necessary to him, though he derives nothing from it except the pleasure of seeing it."

MYTH #5: BUSINESS ETHICS IS AN OXYMORON, A CONTRADICTION

Facebook, YouTube, and other social media companies have argued that they are just a pipeline and are not responsible for the content people put into the pipeline. This attitude has led to public outrage over misogynistic and racist posts, as well as revenge porn, fake news, and attacks on free elections. Social media companies are scrambling to see how they can self-regulate while staying committed to a principle of free speech and expression. Ethics is squarely in the center of the business strategy of these tech giants.

When we mention that we teach "business ethics" to people, either they try not to laugh or they say things like, "Yes, isn't that a contradiction or a theoretical course?" The idea that business and ethics clash has long been a part of the dominant story of business. After all, if business is just about money, shareholders, and profits, there's not much room for ethics as a central part of it. The old narrative pretends that business and ethics can meaningfully be separated.

We have argued that business is concerned with far more than money, profits, and shareholders. By taking into account the effects of business and company actions, we implicitly adopt a point of view that executives should act to bring about the best consequences for all. Of course, money and profits are important, and many business thinkers, such as former GE CEO Jack Welch and business guru Simon Sinek, suggest that we see profits as an outcome of how we manage the entire set of stakeholder relationships.

So too do we have a misconception about ethics. Many people see ethics as completely subjective, believing that each of us has our own "ethics." The question becomes, "Whose ethics do you use?" This question is especially troubling in a multi-stakeholder world. A subjective/individual view of ethics ignores that we share most of our values with others. And we have developed ethical principles in order to solve our conflicts without resorting to violence. There is much more agreement on ethics than there is on many objective issues, such as what counts as good economic performance.

If we believe that business and ethics are separate, then it is likely that capitalism and business will be called into question by society, or business will be seen as a necessary evil. Neither of these alternatives can be sustained in the twenty-first century.

The grain of truth here is that we have, in fact, separated business and ethics. Many of our business models continue to separate the two. Sometimes ethics is simply tacked on to the core business model under the rubric of corporate social responsibility, or seen as a side constraint on what is permissible behavior. Putting business and ethics together at the level of basic business models is a difficult task. And that is precisely what the new story of business, responsible business, seeks to accomplish.

■ ■ ■

Together these myths are a powerful force that strongly resists change. All of us have had conversations with students, executives, or colleagues that demonstrate how strong the traditional story is. Often, a person responds to hearing examples of companies who take purpose, stakeholders, and ethics seriously with remarks like, "Yes, but isn't business really only about the money? Aren't companies only doing these things to make a profit?" We can always reinterpret any behavior as driven by

TABLE 2.1 The Old and New Stories of Business

Dominant Idea	New Story of Business (Chapter 1)
(1) The sole purpose of business is to make profits.	(1) Purpose, values, and ethics are as important as money/profits (Chapter 3).
(2) Business is primarily about serving shareholders, the legitimate "owners" of the business.	(2) Business is about value creation for stakeholders (Chapter 4).
(3) Business works best when allowed to operate in free and unregulated markets.	(3) Business is embedded in society and the physical world (Chapter 5).
(4) Businesspersons are purely economic creatures.	(4) People are complex (Chapter 6).
(5) Business and ethics should be separated.	(5) Business and ethics must be integrated into holistic business models (Chapter 7).

self-interest. It's important to look for credible behavioral signals and commitments before we change our beliefs. But the traditional story of business prevents us from accepting any evidence that businesses care about anything other than profits. It also makes it impossible to believe that better business practices are possible because we recast any efforts toward improvement as driven by narrow self-interest. We are at an inflection point in the history of business and capitalism. It is time to think broadly and creatively about how we can bring out the best in our businesses and businesspeople. The old story of business has become increasingly harmful. It leads to a suffocating regulatory regime, a morally suspect idea about the very nature of business, and a view of people that is unworthy of the dignity and respect that we owe to each other as humans. It's time for a new story, as depicted alongside these old myths in Table 2.1. It's time to do the work that develops the theory and practice of responsible business. We turn to that task in the chapters that follow.

Chapter 3

PURPOSE AND PROFITS

PURPOSE, VALUES, AND ETHICS ARE AS IMPORTANT AS MONEY/PROFITS

Key Ideas

- An increased focus on short-term profits has led to an increase in unethical behavior that has imposed heavy costs to other stakeholders.
- Profit and purpose hang together in our best businesses.
- Having a purpose as a business that is consistent with the ethics and values of the participants in the business draws a great deal of its power from its ability to inspire others.
- One of the main reasons that purpose inspires people is that it makes them a part of something bigger than themselves.

EVEN WALL STREET GETS THE NEW STORY

In his annual letter to CEOs, Blackrock CEO Larry Fink wrote about the current challenging business environment that expects companies to help solve important societal issues. He writes:[1]

> Every company needs a framework to navigate this difficult landscape and that it must begin with a clear embodiment of your company's purpose in your business model and corporate strategy. Purpose is not a mere tagline or marketing campaign; it is a company's fundamental reason for being— what it does every day to create value for its stakeholders. Purpose is not the sole pursuit of profits but the animating force for achieving them.
>
> Profits are in no way inconsistent with purpose—in fact, profits and purpose are inextricably linked. Profits are essential if a company is to effectively serve all of its stakeholders over time—not only shareholders, but also employees, customers, and communities. Similarly, when a company truly understands and expresses its purpose, it functions with the focus and strategic discipline that drive long-term profitability. Purpose unifies management, employees, and communities. It drives ethical behavior and creates an essential check on actions that go against the best interests of stakeholders. Purpose guides culture, provides a framework for consistent decision-making, and, ultimately, helps sustain long-term financial returns for the shareholders of your company.

The new story of business that involves purpose, values, and ethics is beginning to be realized even on Wall Street, as Blackrock, State Street, and other investment houses have gotten the message that purpose counts. Individual companies have long seen the connection between purpose and profits, between caring about the long-term consequences of their actions and the continued short-term health of a business. Consider the following examples:

(1) Toyota has recently reemphasized its purpose, focusing on the idea of the "future of mobility." This new purpose-driven framework provides them with more direction and clarity when making strategic decisions, especially when investigating prospective new markets. Overall, it helps Toyota focus on a significant issue facing the world and develop solutions to tackle it rather than just have them simply identify as an automaker.[2] This conceptual adjustment coincides with their large vision of "Mobility for All" with key partners, International Olympic Committee and the International Paralympic Committee, which is spurring innovation in mobility-based products and services outside of their traditional auto manufacturing sector.[3]

Toyota additionally focuses on environmental leadership. They promise to meet six Environmental Challenge 2050 goals. These involve sustainable solutions to be implemented by their facilities and manufacturing process to significantly reduce CO_2 emissions, reduce water use, recycle to eliminate waste, and be in overall harmony with nature. They have partnered with two nonprofits to help them accomplish these goals: National Public Lands Day and the Wyland Foundation.[4]

Safety is paramount with Toyota as well. It spends millions on research, shares its software and data with partner organizations, and sponsors a program for teen driving education.[5] Called "Teen Drive 365," the program has enrolled approximately 1.5 million teens since its inception. Toyota sponsors this program in partnership with Discovery Education.[6]

(2) Barry-Wehmiller, an industrial machinery manufacturer based in Saint Louis, Missouri, states its purpose as "building a better world through business." Its chairman and CEO, Bob Chapman, states: "Through our business model we have transformed a struggling 100-year-old company into a vibrant global organization committed to creating long-term value for all of our stakeholders."[7]

A Barry-Wehmiller sponsored blog by Chapman, titled "Truly Human Leadership: Transforming Lives Through People-centric Leadership," focuses on sharing the "privilege of leadership," why "everyone matters," and imagining "a world in which people leave work each day fulfilled."[8] The company's BW Leadership Institute offers senior leader training and consulting services to leadership at other businesses. The training's main goal is to infuse in attendees "the overriding purpose of measuring success by the way we touch the lives of people," rather than adopting a profit-driven mindset.[9]

In a recent article on investing in employees to yield better results, Chapman's leadership approach is highlighted. Chapman emphasizes respect for employees and being a good steward to them, and he is quoted as saying, "When somebody comes into our organization and agrees to join us, when we invite them into our organization, we become stewards of that life. And the way we treat that person will profoundly affect that person's marriage and the way that person raises their children and interacts with our community."[10] It is also noted that his company has grown profitably to over $2 billion with this purpose-driven approach. This resiliency was particularly important with the economic downturn in 2009, when Barry-Wehmiller realized a 40 percent drop in new equipment orders—but was able to rebound and see record earnings in 2010.[11]

(3) Started by two brothers in Costa Rica in 1908 and with U.S. headquarters in Rochester, New York, FIFCO is a $1B food and beverage company that brews beer brands such as Imperial, Labatt, and Genesee. FIFCO's motto, "Brands and Breweries with a Purpose," aligns with their purpose-driven mission, which explicitly mentions the importance of their responsibility "to not only grow our business but to also improve the neighborhoods where we work and make a positive contribution to our environment." They espouse the triple bottom line approach to business and emphasize the importance of interrelatedness between the company and their stakeholders— "By connecting with our community and caring for our environment, we have an opportunity to connect with our customers and build our business."[12]

A recent initiative in Costa Rica that exemplifies FIFCO's purpose-driven approach is the company's efforts to lessen their environmental impact by reducing plastic use and waste in their operations, as well as encouraging consumers of their beverages to recycle. The initiative is part of a 2020 goal to recover

100 percent of any plastic FIFCO uses in production, though they are simultaneously working to remove plastic entirely from production. FIFCO is currently recovering 77 percent of their produced plastic as of February 2019.[13]

(4) CarMax has disrupted the automotive business by relying on a sense of purpose. CarMax started in 1993 in Richmond, Virginia, as a side project of Circuit City (code named "Honest Rick's Used Cars" internally[14]). The idea was to have a national, trustworthy brand for purchasing used cars. CarMax states, "Our purpose is to drive integrity in the automotive industry by being honest and transparent in every interaction." Furthermore, it adds key values that spell out how they intend to apply this purpose, stating, "CarMax is built on a foundation of integrity. Our culture is defined by values like respect and transparency. We live these values every day. They drive how we treat our customers and our associates." By relying on purpose, values, and ethics, the company has built a reputation for fair and honest dealing in a business that had become tarnished by a reputation for shady transactions. In 2018, CarMax grossed $17B in sales.

Each of the preceding examples demonstrates the changing way of how we understand business. No longer can we see business as driven purely by concerns of profit—as necessary as profit is. Business is nuanced. Profit and purpose go hand in hand in our best, most resilient businesses. Purpose is buttressed by a sense of values and ethics that determine the legitimacy of any particular purpose. Next, let's take a brief look at the evolution of the purpose of business.

THE PURPOSE OF BUSINESS: A BRIEF HISTORY

The modern business corporation emerged during the twentieth century as one of the most important innovations in human history.[15] Previously, during the 1800s, most businesses were owned and run by families or small groups. These closely held or private companies had a few shareholders who were active in the day-to-day running of the business. By the 1900s, public companies started to appear, with thousands of shareholders who each owned a small fraction of their company's shares. These investors were unable to be involved in the daily activities of the business. In early public companies, such as AT&T, RCA, and GE, the board of directors controlled the company and made key decisions.[16]

When stock speculation caused the market crash of 1929 in the United States, leading to the Great Depression, a debate about the proper purpose of public companies emerged. Was their purpose to make as much money as possible for their thousands of shareholders or to serve a broader purpose? In 1932, the debate was carried out in the *Harvard Law Review*, where Adolph Berle argued for a singular focus on profits for shareholders, and Merrick Dodd argued for a broader purpose that included benefits to customers, employees, and society. Berle eventually conceded the argument, and for the next forty years, Dodd's broader view became the foundation for how society thought about business. Business leaders saw themselves as stewards of public institutions, responsible for a broader group of stakeholders. For example, Bill Hewlett and Dave Packard had a broad purpose when they founded HP in the 1930s. As Dave Packard said to a group of HP managers in March, 1960:[17]

> I think many people assume, wrongly, that a company exists simply to make money. While this is an important result of a company's existence, we have to go deeper and find the real reasons for our being. As we investigate this, we inevitably come to the conclusion that a group of people get together and exist as an institution that we call a company so they are able to accomplish something collectively which they could not accomplish separately. They are able to do something worthwhile—they make a contribution to society (a phrase which sounds trite but is fundamental).

During this period, called "managerial capitalism," business was conducted in a way that reflected the view that size and stability mattered more than growth—managers sat on top of large hierarchies of huge conglomerates and mostly retained and reinvested their earnings.[18] For a while, both workers and executives saw their incomes grow in tandem.[19]

In the late 1960s and early 1970s, the debates about corporate purpose resurfaced as several factors changed the business landscape. First, the size of conglomerates made it hard for headquarters to accurately understand how to create value for each specific business; this led to suboptimal decision making. Second, increased competition from Germany and Japan made U.S. companies less profitable. Third, institutional investors were holding more shares and thus were able to exercise more power over companies than individual shareholders had in the past.

In 1965, for example, 85 percent of shares were owned directly by individuals or households; today, that number is close to 25 percent. Finally, the era of stagflation or rising prices and high unemployment threatened U.S. prosperity.[20] Economists and policymakers began looking for a way to jump-start it.

To get the U.S. economy back on track, economists argued that executives should focus on shareholders and profits as part of a return to economic efficiency. Economists Milton Friedman, Michael Jensen, and others argued that shareholders needed more control over managers who used their power to build and maintain their empires and feather their nests rather than to compete in the global economy. As an example, Fred Borsch, the CEO of GE, pledged a renewed focus on the "forgotten" shareholder.[21]

The 1980s marked the transition from managerial capitalism to investor capitalism. It ushered in a wave of corporate takeovers in which large conglomerates were bought, broken up, and sold off in pieces to increase shareholder returns. Eventually, in the 1990s, CEO compensation became increasingly tied to share price. In 1965, the average CEO made 44 times more than the average worker. Today, that number is close to 370 times, with stock-based compensation making up a third of what the average CEO makes.[22] Of course, part of the reason for this was a law passed by Congress in 1993 that encouraged the use of stock options as compensation.

As companies were increasingly evaluated primarily on their ability to produce short-term earnings, some executives responded to that pressure by laying off workers, outsourcing production, buying back shares, cutting R&D expenses, and taking unethical shortcuts to raise the share price. An increased focus on short-term results led to an increase in corporate scandals, the global financial crisis, and unethical behavior that imposed heavy costs on other stakeholders. The result has been a variety of proposals for reform, ironically leading to calls for a more responsible idea of business. In short, purpose matters. Focusing on shareholder value as the sole purpose of a company has led us to a crisis of capitalism and has produced less resilient companies who struggle through adversity. Thankfully, the landscape is changing.

PURPOSE IN BUSINESS: WHAT IS IT?

A core idea of purpose is the simple notion of having a goal. But consider the variety of businesses that exist in the world. Purpose answers questions such as "Why does this business exist?" "What difference is it trying to make in the world, and why should people care?" In the words of John Mackey and Raj Sisodia, coauthors of *Conscious Capitalism* (one of the new models of business): "A firm's purpose is the glue that holds the organization together, the amniotic fluid that nourishes the life force of the organization. You can also think of it as a magnet that attracts the right people—the right team members, customers, suppliers, and investors—to the business and aligns them."[23]

In the words of David Cruickshank, Deloitte Global Chairman, "This exemplifies a shift in the relationship between purpose and profit. They no longer have to be adversarial priorities—purpose and profit can coexist within the same business strategy."[24]

Purpose, however, cannot stand alone. While there is a general idea in business that a purpose is a good thing, we have too many examples of organizations whose purpose is anything but good. White supremacist organizations, rogue states, terrorist organizations, and organized crime also have purposes. Purpose needs to also be in touch with societal and ethical values, ruling out as illegitimate those that depend on intolerance and those that deny basic humanity to all.

That said, we will discuss the concepts of purpose, values, and ethics as interconnected.

There are many different interpretations of values and ethics. We use these terms in their most basic sense. At the personal level values are the drivers, the reasons for our actions and behaviors. They express our desires and preferences. Our values are connected to our history and our relationships with others. Values require reflection and introspection. Values also express our aspirations. We don't always act on our values, and sometimes we make mistakes. Our values express how we act at our very best, even though there can be barriers, including our own weaknesses, to such action.

In business, values can serve the same function, as reasons for behavior and action. When a company states that one of its values is "caring for its people," it expresses a way of seeing its employees as humans worthy of compassion, as well as an aspiration to care about them. Organizational values can answer such questions as, "Why are we doing what we are doing?" "How are we going to work together?" "For whom are we creating value?"

We can think about ethics as a set of individual and societal values that frame how we interact with each other. We can also think about ethics as a set of principles or rules for such interaction. There is no need to solve age-old philosophical problems in understanding the narrative of responsible business. It is enough to point out that these new models connect business with purpose, values, and ethics.

Purpose often emerges from our values and ethics and is always connected to them. This is an especially good place to start for a company that seems to be purposeless or one in search of its purpose. Founded in 1993 in Alexandria, Virginia, Motley Fool is a financial services company that focuses on providing financial advice. When Motley Fool states its purpose as "To Help the World Invest Better," it is expressing values, some of which are ethical or moral values. It goes on to state its values in the following way:

- Be foolish.
- Collaborate: Do great things together.
- Innovate: Search for a better solution. Then top it.
- Fun: Revel in your work.
- Honest: Make us proud.
- Competitive: Play fair, play hard, play to win.
- Motley: Make foolishness your own. Share your core value_____.

These values include an implicit idea of a human as a fun-loving, hard-working, ethical, collaborative, innovative, and individual creature capable of doing great things. Motley Fool's idea is that people can bring their own values to the workplace and align them with the company's values. Gardner tells the story of how Motley Fool's values evolved:[25]

> It was sort of a 10-year look back on our values. How much are we living by them? Are these the values that we believe in? Do we have the wording for the values? And are we expressing them and communicating them in our organization from somebody's first week at the company all the way through to their twentieth year at the company? How well are we doing? And that group came back with five or six recommendations, and one of those recommendations was the creation of our sixth value, which we call our "motley value"; and, as you said, that's the value that you name for yourself.
>
> . . . If you can bring your own value, you're looking at how that value fits into the other values of the company, so now you're connecting with those values, and evaluating which ones you think you live up to and which ones are challenges for you, so it has elevated the relevance of the values in our culture.

PURPOSE, ETHICS, AND VALUES INSPIRE PEOPLE

A business purpose consistent with the ethics and values of the participants is a powerful inspiration. Indeed, ordinary people are inspired by purpose to do quite extraordinary things. As humans, we want to be part of something bigger than ourselves. We are social creatures and want to join groups that can accomplish more than we can do alone, connecting them to organizations and tasks they want to participate in. Purpose helps us make a difference in the world.

Mackey and Sisodia believe that the new story of business needs purposes beyond merely making profits. They point out what they call "higher purpose," by which they mean something beyond just making money. For example, Medtronic's purpose was more than making money. Indeed, as one of the largest medical device companies in the world, its purpose even went beyond prolonging life. The founder met with new employees and told them the purpose of Medtronic was to allow people to lead a full life. This became a life-long, inspirational memory for employees.[26]

Research also supports this idea. Wharton scholar Adam Grant found that when employees were presented with the prosocial outcomes of their work—for example, fundraisers in a call center who were motivated by the benefits to students of their fundraising efforts—they outperformed others who were less prosocially motivated. Grant found that "callers with high levels of both prosocial and intrinsic motivations averaged 51.82 calls and $510.58 in donations as compared with an average of 40.26 calls and $308.10 in donations for the other callers."[27]

A survey of CEOs and employees at 520 companies[28] in seventeen countries found that when CEOs emphasized economic values, followers were likely to perceive them as autocratic. However, when CEOs emphasized stakeholder values, followers were more likely to perceive them as visionary leaders. When employees saw their leaders as visionary, they expended more effort at work, and their companies saw increased financial performance. Humans need meaning; when employees find their work meaningful, tangible business outcomes result, such as reduced absenteeism and stress, as well as increased motivation, engagement, and job satisfaction.[29]

PURPOSE DRIVES ENTREPRENEURS

We have talked to hundreds of entrepreneurs and would-be entrepreneurs over several decades. Rarely do we find entrepreneurs motivated solely by the big payoff. Starting a business and working to make it successful is simply too difficult. It is easier to make money by working a steady job. Most entrepreneurs are simply passionate about an idea, one they can clearly see, even if the rest of the world cannot. Their purpose is to bring that idea to life and to get others to experience it the way that they do. Purpose is simply a better way to think about what entrepreneurs actually do.

Claus Meyer, the founder of NOMA restaurant in Denmark, said "we didn't start NOMA to make money because we didn't make any for the first 19 years."[30] Bill Curtis, owner and operator of Tastings restaurant in Charlottesville, Virginia, just wants to bring the joy of good French country cooking and good wine to people in his community. The entrepreneurs at Red Goat Records are driven by their love of original rhythm and blues music and are determined to bring the joy of it to more people in the twenty-first century.[31]

There are literally thousands of examples of entrepreneurs driven by purpose. Of course, these businesses—from large multinationals to small start-ups—must also make profits if they are to continue to exist, but seeing business as primarily a profit-making enterprise does not do justice to the reality of business life.

In the words of entrepreneur and Whole Foods Market cofounder and CEO John Mackey,

> Most entrepreneurs start businesses because they are on fire about an idea. Very few of them start a business solely to make money, except of course in economics textbooks. I have known hundreds of entrepreneurs in my life. With only a few exceptions, entrepreneurs didn't start their businesses to maximize profits for shareholders. Of course they wanted to make money, but that's not what was driving them. What was driving them in most cases was some kind of passion. They were on fire about something. It could be like Bill Gates wanting to create software to do the personal computer revolution. It could be the passion I felt with Whole Foods to sell healthy, organic, natural food to people. . . . The entrepreneur who creates the business is the first one to determine what the purpose of the business is.[32]

■ ■ ■

Purpose is powerful, especially when connected to a set of ethical values that define how the business wants to operate in order to realize its purpose. Purpose has to be connected to virtually everything that an organization does and how it creates value for its stakeholders.

There is skepticism around the idea that businesses can and do have a purpose greater than profits. Part of this skepticism comes from the persistent grip of the old story of business. And a certain degree of skepticism is justified, as sometimes businesses articulate a purpose but don't follow through on the hard work that purpose entails. A business truly can be said to be purpose-driven only if the purpose lives in the everyday actions and the systems and processes of a business. And when an employee or other stakeholder begins to question whether or not a company is living its purpose, such pushback needs to be welcomed as a way to ensure that the purpose is alive and well. In other words, talk is cheap.

We can see how far off track companies can get when they focus solely on growth and profits. Facebook's focus for the past ten years has been growth in the name of profits (Facebook even has a vice president of growth). But growing the user base is important to sell access to their actual customers—advertising companies. In fact, the only customers listed in their annual reports are advertisers. The focus on growth in the name of profits has led them down the path of discriminatory advertising, manipulative political campaigns, and the tracing of users across platforms—and, not surprisingly, congressional hearings. Their former chief of security left and has become a vocal advocate for the protection of user data.[33] On the other hand, companies such as Change.org (creation of campaigns by users), Vote.org (increase voter turnout), and Pigeonly.com (affordable communications for inmates with friends and family) use technology for a specific purpose without sacrificing integrity for short-term profits.

Chapter 4

STAKEHOLDERS AND SHAREHOLDERS

BUSINESS IS ABOUT CREATING VALUE FOR STAKEHOLDERS

Key Ideas

- Stakeholders are individuals and groups who can affect the business and be affected by it.
- The myth that companies seek to maximize shareholder value tells an incomplete story.
- Businesses are broadening their purpose and creating value for all stakeholders, including customers, employees, suppliers, financiers, and communities.
- A large and growing body of research supports the idea that managing for stakeholders drives better financial performance and resiliency through adversity.

INTRODUCTION: THE AUSTIN FLOOD

In 1981, a few years after the founding of Whole Foods Market, Austin, Texas, suffered what natives called a "hundred-year flood." At the time of the flood, Whole Foods had one store, and it lost everything in the deluge. As CEO John Mackey tells it, he thought the company was finished—they had no money, no inventory, and not much hope. What the company did have, however, was a commitment from its stakeholders to help get it back on its feet. Customers and community members showed up at the store to urge Mackey and his employees to rebuild. They offered to help, and Mackey was able to secure money from banks, inventory from suppliers, and support from employees, customers, and community members to rebuild the store and the company. It was from this support that Mackey rebuilt Whole Foods Market on what he calls "stakeholder principles."[1]

WHO IS A STAKEHOLDER?

We can define the term *stakeholder* in a number of ways. First, we could define it narrowly as the idea that any business must create value for "those groups without whose support, the business would cease to be viable."[2] In figure 4.1, the inner circle depicts this view. Almost every business is concerned at some level with the relationships among financiers, customers, suppliers, communities, and employees.

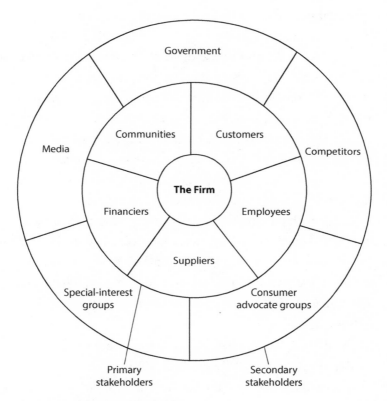

FIGURE 4.1 The firm stakeholders

Source: R. Edward Freeman, Jeffrey Harrison, and Andrew Wicks, *Managing for Stakeholders* (New Haven: Yale University Press, 2007). Provided by the author.

For instance, Colgate Palmolive, a consumer household products company, states, "Each day, the 38,000 employees of Colgate-Palmolive share a commitment to bringing you safe, effective products, as well as programs to enrich communities around the world." They believe in "living our values" and name three: caring, global teamwork, and continuous improvement.[3] They differentiate their stakeholders as Colgate-Palmolive people, customers, shareholders, and business partners. With these stakeholders in mind, they consider their ethical obligations, "Colgate-Palmolive is committed to acting with compassion, integrity, honesty and high ethics in all situations, to listen with respect to others and to value differences. The Company is also committed to protect the global environment, to enhance the communities where Colgate-Palmolive people live and work, and to be compliant with government laws and regulations."[4]

In line with their view, Colgate-Palmolive has many sustainability and community programs. One recent example, with a global footprint, is the Colgate Bright Smiles, Bright Futures® program. Each year, it provides over 50 million children with free dental screens and educational materials focused on healthy habits and self-esteem.[5]

Similarly, Interstate Batteries, a U.S.-based battery manufacturer, states that it is values-driven, not profit-driven: "With our values as a framework, we believe that profits will never drive our success the way our purpose can." In the "Purpose and Values" section of its website it specifically mentions the importance of living its values: "Our values, however, are unchanging, and we ask that our team members try their best to live them as they serve our key stakeholders: team members, customers, distributors and franchisees, suppliers and vendors, communities and shareholders. By creating a welcoming and caring environment, we hope to create a positive experience for our team members and everyone else whom Interstate touches, no matter their background or belief system."[6] To Colgate-Palmolive and

Interstate Batteries, to focus solely on maximizing shareholder wealth would be incomplete.

A broader definition of *stakeholder* captures the idea that if a group or individual can affect a business, then the executives must take that group into consideration in thinking about how to create value. Put another way, a stakeholder is any group or individual who can affect or be affected by the realization of an organization's purpose.

Research shows that the use of the term *stakeholder* began in the 1960s at the Stanford Research Institute and in Sweden, even though the underlying idea can be found in a number of texts, businesses, and societies. Initially, the idea of stakeholders was used in a business's strategic planning process to organize information about the external environment. As the 1980s progressed, businesses became interested in using the stakeholder idea to delineate corporate responsibilities. Eventually, business models emerged that used the stakeholder idea as their very basic unit of analysis. Business models began to be seen as expressions of how a business created value for its stakeholders. Most large companies and many smaller ones articulate the groups and individuals that they create value for. The stakeholder idea has become a regular part of our language of business.

CREATING VALUE FOR STAKEHOLDERS

The basic idea of creating value for stakeholders is quite simple, as shown in figure 4.1: business can be understood as a set of relationships among groups and individuals who have a stake in the activities that make up the business. Business is about how customers, suppliers, employees, financiers (stockholders, bond-holders, banks, and so on), communities, and managers interact and create value. To understand a business is to know how these relationships work. The executive's or entrepreneur's job is to manage these relationships.

Another way to see this point is to ask, "What makes any business successful and sustainable over time?" The answer from a practical point of view is that it continuously creates value for its customers, suppliers, employees, financiers, and communities (including civil society). If it loses the support of any one of these groups, over time and in a free society, that group could use the political process to enforce its perceived claims. Business is a voluntary activity—for the most part. Those who engage with a business do so voluntarily, since they usually have some amount of choice about whether or not to do so. Of course, the degree of choice depends on the underlying structure of society and markets.

This is not to say the singular focus on maximizing share-holder value, normally through immediate profit maximiza-tion, is not a guiding story. In fact, one argument in favor of managers focusing on short-term profit maximization is that it is *easier* than creating value for stakeholders: if we give execu-tives and managers a single goal that is easy to measure (such as maximizing shareholder value), their job is supposedly simpler. But maximizing shareholder wealth is only part of the story, and it allows companies to miss opportunities, value creation, and interests in other stakeholder relationships. So attractive is the old myth that early in the development of our version of stakeholder theory, around 1978, Freeman and James Emshoff sent a working paper to a journal to be listed. A representative of the journal called to confirm the journal would list the paper but then said "there is a typo in the title. It says 'stakeholder management,' and we know you meant 'stockholder management.' Don't worry; we will change it for you."

Any business must create some value for its customers with products and services that improve their lives so that customers are willing to pay for that value. Any business must work with suppliers as their customers for the same reasons. Moreoer, customer and supplier relationships are enmeshed in ethics. Companies make promises to customers via their advertising, and when products or services don't deliver on these promises, then management has a responsibility to rectify the situation, or customers will remove support. It is important to have suppliers committed to improving a company. If suppliers find a better, faster, and cheaper way of making critical parts or services, then both supplier and company can win. Of course, some suppliers simply compete on price, but even so, there is a moral element of fairness and transparency to the supplier relationship.

Many customers simply love Apple, Inc. Its products are simply designed and easy to use. Apple emphasizes creating value for customers, but they also cannot ignore suppliers who are a vital part of the stakeholder value creation chain. After a great deal of criticism over the way some Apple suppliers treated employees, the company analyzed how it created value for its suppliers. In Apple's 2019 Supplier Responsibility Progress Report, Tim Cook (CEO) states, "We believe that business, at its best, serves the public good, empowers people around the world, and binds us together as never before."Their motto, written multiple times in large bold font is, "People come first. In everything we do." The report highlights their programs to meet or exceed internationally recognized standards and principles related to responsible mining of resources and human rights. It describes how the company spends resources on educating their workforce through training and work-study programs, often in underdeveloped areas of the world. Apple also reports the results of the audits and assessments conducted by their suppliers and third-party entities to ensure transparency and take corrective action when needed. When implementing these programs to meet their goals, they also mention the importance of working across sectors (e.g., government, civil society).[7]

Businesses must create value for employees so they are willing to learn how to operate the business. This is especially true in the twenty-first century with many routine tasks now completed by machines or artificial intelligence (AI). Employee jobs and livelihoods are often at stake. Employees often have specialized skills for which there is usually no perfectly elastic market. In return for their labor, they expect security, wages, benefits, and meaningful work. Often employees are expected to participate in the decision-making of the organization, and if the employees are management or senior executives, we see them as shouldering a great deal of responsibility for the conduct of the entire organization. Research makes it clear that the more employees are engaged in the business, the more successful the business.[8]

SAP, a German company that designs and develops enterprise software for businesses, has several ongoing programs to engage employees. In 2019, a partnership grants program was available for designated urban areas to improve "computer science education and building a diverse workforce." In addition, it encourages its employees to volunteer through company initiatives. For example, SAP launched a "Spring into Service" campaign in 2017 that allowed employees to develop and implement their own service projects that resulted in more than ten thousand employees contributing 41,000 volunteer hours in cities worldwide.[9] Another significant focus of SAP is its SAP One Billion Lives (1BL) social entrepreneurship initiative.[10] Executive Board Member of SAP SE, Adaire Fox-Martin, discusses the importance of bringing the "company's purpose to life" through this initiative. Reinforcing her belief that "humanity is inherently good," this initiative draws on SAP employees' talents and technology expertise for social entrepreneurship. They are developing what they refer to as "intrapreneurship," fostering an entrepreneurial mindset for CSR-related endeavors.[11]

Businesses must create value for their financiers. To say that stakeholders are important is not to deny the importance of shareholders, bondholders, banks, and others who seem to have a purely "financial" stake in the business. These stakes will differ by type of owner, preferences for time horizon, moral preferences, and so forth, as well as by type of business. Importantly, even if the leaders of a business care only about maximizing value for shareholders, they must still balance diverse shareholder factions. Do we pay attention to long-term shareholders or shareholders who want to flip the stock? The shareholders of Google may well want returns as well as to be supportive of Google's articulated purpose of "don't be evil." Growing markets for social impact investing take shareholders' broader values into account; indeed, this is one of the new models of business that we mentioned in chapter 1. For example, more than one dollar out of every five invested in the United States goes through some kind of screen in the market for socially responsible investing, which has grown by leaps and bounds to well over $30 trillion. However, focusing on financiers as the only stakeholder tells an incomplete story of business.

Satori Capital is a private equity firm based in Dallas, Texas, that wants what is best for its investors, and it believes that conscious capitalism companies are best suited to give the best returns to investors. It inculcates a "Sustainable Mindset" into its culture. Satori espouses the idea of conscious capitalism as interchangeable with the concept of sustainability. The company believes so strongly in this mindset and a stakeholder-based approach that they include the following in every investor agreement: "We also believe that sustainably run businesses are more innovative, less risky, and better positioned for growth because all stakeholders have a vested interest in the success of the company."[12] Throughout their entire partnership with the companies they have invested in, Satori Capital emphasizes the need for the company to take a purpose-driven, long-term, and stakeholder-centric perspective in all their strategic decisions. This encapsulates their conscious capital approach, which avoids the notion of putting profits first and short-term thinking.[13]

It is controversial to say that business must create value for communities, but it is nonetheless true. The local community grants firms the right to build facilities and use public resources such as roads and infrastructure. In turn, it benefits from the tax base and the economic and social contributions of the firm. Companies have a real impact on communities, and being located in a welcoming community helps a company create value for its other stakeholders. In return for the provision of local services, companies are expected to be good citizens. A company should not expose the community to unreasonable hazards in the form of pollution, toxic waste, and so forth. It should honor whatever commitments it makes and make sure it operates in as transparent a manner as possible. Communities often speak out via the regulatory process or the courts and prevent a particular business from operating within their boundaries. More often, communities have sought restitution when a business has damaged a community, even if it had the government's permission to inflict the damage.

Cisco Systems, based in San Jose, California, manufactures networking hardware and telecommunications equipment. The company sells to the high tech market. In 2018, Cisco promised to donate $50 million to fight chronic homelessness in Santa Clara County (where Cisco is headquartered) with a public-private partnership called "Destination: Home."[14] In that same year, they donated another $10 million, along with the public companies LinkedIn and Pure Storage, to invest in a community development financial institution (CDFI) whose purpose is to provide affordable housing in the notoriously expensive San Francisco Bay region. Chuck Robbins, chairman and CEO, said of the initiative, "Partnering with other organizations gives us the ability to create an even greater impact. We are excited to join the leaders from Pure Storage and LinkedIn to increase the capacity of the TECH Fund because we recognize the scale of the local housing crisis and the impact this solution can have in increasing the availability of affordable housing."[15]

Executives play a special role in the activity of a business enterprise. They have a stake like every other employee regarding an actual or implied employment contract that is linked to the stakes of financiers, customers, suppliers, communities, and other employees. They are also expected to look after the health of the overall enterprise to keep the various stakes moving in roughly the same direction and to maintain balance. Executives can't focus on their own comfort and benefit but need to focus instead on creating value for others.

The interests of each stakeholder do not exist in isolation. How engaged your employees are surely affects your ability to innovate and produce quality products for your customers, and there are similarities among all stakeholders. There is now a burgeoning and substantial literature on how stakeholder interests affect all areas of business.[16] The introduction of this simple and practical idea of creating value for stakeholders, together with the idea that there are multiple possible purposes for businesses, large and small, turns the old narrative on its head.

Research shows that firms that adopt responsible social and environmental practices experience less financial volatility, higher sales growth, and a better chance of survival compared to a carefully matched control group. Importantly, these firms showed no difference in short-term profits.[17] The authors argue socially responsible or sustainable practices help firms avoid crises and rebound from external shocks. Strong organizational stakeholder networks allow firms to better withstand financial, environmental, and other shocks by working within their stakeholder relationships: the idea is that, to show resiliency in adversity, a company is stronger in a group rather than in isolation.[18]

In a recent book reflecting on his experience as CEO of the Medtronic Company, a medical technology and services company, Bill George summarized the creating-value-for-stakeholders mindset:[19]

> Serving all your stakeholders is the best way to produce long-term results and create a growing and prosperous company . . . let me be very clear about this. There is no conflict between serving all your stakeholders and providing excellent returns for shareholders. In the long term, it is impossible to have one without the other. However, serving all the stakeholder groups requires discipline, vision, and committed leadership.

THE PRIMACY OF STAKEHOLDER RELATIONSHIPS, NOT TRANSACTIONS

A useful unit of analysis of business is simply the set of stakeholder relationships rather than discrete economic transactions. Most businesses consist of the voluntary cooperation of at least the following entities: customers, suppliers, employees, communities (including civil society), and financiers. This collaborative system includes agreements that extend over time based on fairness and trust, rather than merely transaction by transaction. Value is created for each stakeholder because each can freely agree to cooperate with the others. By looking at a large group of stakeholder relationships, rather than a single transaction, executives can better understand the effects of managerial decisions on a broader system of relationships. This is important because it allows us to create ways to make decisions that benefit the ecosystem of stakeholder relationships, rather than trying to maximize a particular variable within a transaction and then causing value-destroying consequences in other areas.

The key difference is that in a relationship, there is a presumption that the relationship will continue over time, other things being equal. Businesses need loyal relationships with stakeholders. Seeing these relationships through the lens of "discrete transactions unrelated to each other" does not build loyalty. In fact, it encourages exit when things get tough. Building loyalty with stakeholders mitigates the risks of difficult times, as John Mackey discovered with the Austin flood.

Of course, relationships are two-way streets. Companies have to stand by their suppliers and employees when times are tough for them. Furthermore, they have to share in the rewards of success in a broad manner, not just in terms of rewarding senior management.

STAKEHOLDER INTERESTS ARE INTERCONNECTED

Stakeholder interests are interconnected. For instance, employee well-being is connected to customer well-being. Each stakeholder contributes to the value created for the others. And rarely is this process reducible to mere transactions or contracts. The executive's task is to continuously work to get stakeholder interests moving in the same direction. This works best when executives see the interdependence among stakeholders. This interdependence requires a set of skills and ideas that use our creative imagination. This is best exercised in full engagement with the stakeholders themselves. Stakeholder engagement is sometimes thought to be another way to achieve corporate social responsibility. However, the idea is much more comprehensive. Stakeholder engagement is really about how a particular firm's business model creates value for all of its stakeholders.

One common way of framing stakeholder interests is in terms of trade-offs among different stakeholder groups. Economists love trade-offs.[20] One of the hallmarks of modern economics is that trade-offs can always be calculated. We have become increasingly skeptical of trade-off thinking. Actually, the drive to avoid it by collaborating is quite powerful. When we see the task of the executive as getting stakeholder interests pointing in the same direction over time, trade-offs will disappear. Of course, sometimes they must be made because we can't imagine an alternative, but when we make a trade-off we need to immediately begin the process of making that trade-off better for both sides.

To illustrate, consider the case of a large chemical company that decided to commit to being more sustainable and cleaner. The CEO announced a lofty sustainability goal. He then visited the various divisions and plant sites to let managers and employees know that he was serious and to lay out interim goals and plans. In one facility, as he told the story to a symposium at Dartmouth in the 1990s, the engineers came up to him and said, "Sorry, but we can't meet these interim goals. This process is too dirty, this equipment is too old, and we can't meet the first target." The CEO responded that they would have to close the plant. What we understood from that was that he was willing, however reluctantly, to make a trade-off, environment/community on the one hand versus employees on the other. The CEO's trade-off was that the environment was a serious issue and it was going to prevail. So, he told the engineers to prepare to close the plant. A few weeks later, the engineers announced that a miracle had occurred. They had figured out how to meet the goals without closing the plant, thus avoiding a trade-off. When the CEO asked what it would cost, the engineers actually were embarrassed to say that the new method would save money.

When trade-off thinking becomes unacceptable, we kick into gear the only infinite resource we really have, which is our creative imagination. The use of creative imagination is radically underused in most companies today. Making trade-offs is usually easier than doing the hard work of applying one's creative imagination, but in the new story of business and its stakeholder mindset, trade-offs become managerial failures. As increasingly more companies consider the new story of business, they discover ways to satisfy multiple stakeholders. If purpose is also at the center of a business's thinking, then it becomes easier to engage in win-win behavior. Thus if an entrepreneur or an executive can find a purpose that speaks to the core value of the firm as well as to the hearts and minds of key stakeholders, it is more likely to gain sustained success.

What this means is that conflict, often avoided in many companies, is precisely the place where value creation can take place. Where there's conflict among stakeholders, where there's conflict among core values, where there's conflict among competitors or products, this is exactly the place where we can reimagine that conflict and create value. We have to come to see conflict as a good thing. For example, Company X was the target of a campaign by a global nongovernmental organization (NGO) because of its practices in the Amazon rainforest. The executives in Company X saw this campaign as an opportunity to work with the NGO to get better practices on this issue. In fact, the NGO actually helped them solve an operational problem that led to much more value being created.

Seeing and facilitating the interconnectedness of stakeholder interests and avoiding trade-off thinking is the essence of the art of management in the new story of business. No company is better at this than John Mackey's Whole Foods Market. The company recognizes the importance of getting feedback from multiple stakeholder groups. When developing standards for high-quality products, it takes a multi-stakeholder view with the goal of being, as Whole Foods Market's Carrie Brownstein blogged, "the leader in responsible sourcing of food and other products, [as] our stakeholders challenge us to aim high." They do not take a rigid process for their multi-stakeholder approach, which can consist of forums, meetings, emails, and so on, that aim to bring all of the key stakeholders in on the decision-making process. Even though this multi-stakeholder framework can be a lot more work, the company finds it worthwhile. According to Brownstein, "Running a multi-stakeholder process is a lot of work, but it's worth it in the end because when our stakeholders are involved in the process of developing standards, they're invested in the outcome and can share in the success."[21]

THE RESEARCH ON THE STAKEHOLDER APPROACH

Over the last twenty-five years, there has been a growing body of research on the idea of managing for stakeholders, and the findings are increasingly clear. Empirical evidence consistently suggests that companies that focus on creating value for stakeholders perform better financially than those that focus only on maximizing shareholder value. For example, companies that are regularly included on Fortune's Best Places to Work list outperform competitors by 2 to 4 percent.[22] That may seem like a small percentage, but when you compare it to the growth of the S&P 500 over the last ten years (7.7 percent), it is pretty compelling. Similarly, companies that rank high in customer satisfaction outperform competitors by 7 to 8 percent, and companies that are good stewards of the environment outperform competitors by 4 to 6 percent.[23] All of these benefits do not even take into account the losses and costs of a damaging public scandal. During the last forty years, hundreds of studies have been conducted on the relationship between broader stakeholder management and financial performance, and these studies have converged on a modest performance benefit (3 to 7 percent) for companies that focus on creating value for stakeholders. The specific size of the performance benefit varies by industry, time period, and the specific companies sampled. For example, a recent McKinsey study found that companies managed for the long term (defined as five to seven years) have 36 percent greater earnings, 47 percent higher revenues, and an increased market capitalization of $7 billion compared to companies focused on the short term.[24] Another study of twenty-eight firms that excel at creating value for their stakeholders found that these companies outperformed the S&P 500 from 1996 through 2006 by 8 to 1.[25]

The results are more compelling when companies within a specific industry or sector are compared. An analysis comparing Walmart (specifically, Sam's Club) and Costco found that the focus of Sam's Club on everyday low prices resulted in it paying a minimum wage, shortening employee hours, and offering minimal health insurance and benefits to employees. On a per-employee basis, Sam's Club paid lower wages than Costco, which paid a wage of $20 an hour.[26] But the story doesn't stop there. Sam's Club has a high turnover (44 percent), which is costly because it has to train new employees. Costco's turnover is less than half that of Sam's Club at 17 percent, which is rare in retail. Additionally, sales per employee are higher at Costco because employees who feel cared for and supported are better at taking care of customers. Research has demonstrated that there is a significant positive effect on employee engagement in companies that focus on serving a broader group of stakeholders.[27] Overall, by paying a higher wage, Costco ends up ahead.

Similarly, a recent study by a team of researchers at the Wharton School showed that positive stakeholder relationships are critical to the success of firms.[28] Conducted in the context of publicly traded gold mines, research by Witold Henisz and his colleagues showed that positive stakeholder relationships, such as support from local government and NGOs, were worth two times the price of mined gold. When a company had a negative stakeholder relationship, such as with a combative union or unsupportive local government, it paid unforeseen costs, like increased waiting time for permits or stalled production because of labor disputes that significantly damaged its profitability.

■ ■ ■

When the stakeholder idea is combined with purpose, values, and ethics, we can harness the power of these new models of business. When stakeholders are galvanized around a purpose, the results are incredible organizational energy and performance. Inspired employees delight customers. Purpose-driven employees and delighted customers can cause suppliers and other partners to innovate. Paying attention to community makes all stakeholders better off. And, if done in the right spirit, this both/and mindset results in benefits for financiers and communities.

Chapter 5

SOCIETY AND MARKETS

BUSINESS IS EMBEDDED IN SOCIETY AND IN A PHYSICAL WORLD

Key Ideas

- As opposed to the myth that business occurs in some mythical free-market utopia where ordinary rules don't apply, it is in fact embedded in society and the physical world.
- Focusing on the dominant narrative that business functions within a free market misses the value created by business in relation to its communities.
- Society is an important factor to all businesses. Firms foster mutually beneficial relationships with their immediate community.
- Business and society work together. Firms partner with societal institutions, such as governments, communities, nonprofits, and universities, to solve problems.

- Business can take on institutional failure. Firms see institutional failures as opportunities and sometimes as targets for activism.

THE PATAGONIA STORY

Patagonia, the popular manufacturer of outdoor clothing such as jackets and vests, donates to causes of interest and is proactive in working with society to understand their impact on the planet. Patagonia helped organize the Sustainable Apparel Coalition with forty-nine members, all of which are dedicated to the goal of "an apparel industry that produces no unnecessary environmental harm and has a positive impact on the people and communities associated with its activities."[1] Patagonia also works to reduce waste in their supply chain and manage the chemicals, dyes, and finishes used in the process of making their clothes.

In 2007, Patagonia started tracking and sharing their social and environmental data with other apparel brands doing business in similar areas. Then, in 2019, Patagonia turned downstream to see how their products were being used, and decided to sell their very popular fleece vests only to "more mission-driven companies that prioritize the planet."[2] This move particularly impacted Wall Street firms, as Patagonia announced it would not supply corporate-branded fleece vests to companies it deemed insufficiently planet-friendly.[3] The company also promoted conscious consumption of clothing through their "don't buy this jacket" ad campaign, which asked consumers to buy only what they needed and to take care of it.

BUSINESS *IN* SOCIETY: WHAT IS HUMAN SOCIETY?

We sometimes envision business as being set in some mythical free-market utopia where ordinary rules don't apply because competition is perfect and the invisible hand is everywhere. But in the real world, the institution of business is set squarely amongst other institutions such as government, public education, families, religious institutions, higher education, and others. Any workable idea about business must take these institutions into account. In this chapter, we explore the manner in which business is situated *in* society, and how companies manage that relationship successfully.

The truth is that business has never only been about free markets, and markets have always been embedded in the rest of society.[4] Successful markets need individuals whose rights are protected, private property that is respected, and contracts that are enforced. Such protection, respect, and enforcement are all provided by societal institutions. Even traders of antiquity created communities to ensure that the norms of trade were respected, and they invested in collective infrastructures, such as roads and security, which had positive externalities for the immediate society. Companies need society, and society relies on businesses for the value they create.

Yet, the alternative—the myth that "business is an island" operating alone in so-called free markets—is sticky and difficult to shake. According to the myth, individuals, as executives, are expected to be interested in looking out solely for themselves, and are consequently assumed to be selfish. We find examples of this myth frequently in finance and economics texts, where businesses are urged to look out for number one and concern themselves with others only if it helps generate more profit.

For example, in 1997, Lehman Brothers and Bear Stearns global investment firms were criticized for not playing a role in saving the financial services industry. A large hedge fund, Long Term Capital Management (LTCM), was not able to uphold its financial commitments, and many other banks relied upon LTCM's ability to pay what they owed. In other words, LTCM's liquidity problem was poised to bring the entire system down. The CEOs of eight banks agreed to put forward $250 million each to shore up the industry for a self-bailout. Lehman Brothers' and Bear Stearns' CEOs, Dick Fuld and Jimmy Cayne respectively, withheld their shares.[5] Despite Bear Stearns being the clearinghouse for most of LTCM's trades, its CEO Jimmy Cayne infamously said "F*** you" when asked to provide a share of the private bailout.[6]

This myth that business is an island, and it's everyone for themselves is bolstered by the false premise that we are not prosocial creatures. Society itself, according to this myth, is a collection of selfish, individual actors, and in business we only care about—and only should care about—surviving and making money. This implicit theory of society as individualistic and selfish is deeply held—at least in the Western world, where it is seen to be a virtue. This comes from a faulty understanding of evolution and human behavior. Richard Dawkin's famous book, *The Selfish Gene*, is a good example of this societal dichotomy, as it pits self-interest against altruism. Dawkins states, "let us try to teach generosity and altruism because we are born selfish. Let us try to understand what our selfish genes are up to," and,

"Any altruistic system is inherently unstable because it is open to abuse by selfish individuals."[7]

In business, we see self-preservation framed as selfishness in the misunderstood invisible hand metaphor. Adam Smith quite famously said in *The Wealth of Nations*, "It is not from the benevolence of the butcher, the brewer, or the baker that we expect our dinner, but from their regard to their own self-interest. We address ourselves not to their humanity but to their self-love, and never talk to them of our own necessities, but of their advantages." This one passage is then used to justify certain outrageously self-serving acts of individuals and companies by claiming that (a) we all act selfishly and (b) society functions best if we act that way. For example, Volkswagen's emission scandal, where the company modified its computer program so that the car activated its emissions controls during but then reverted to heavy during actual driving, is justified by this flawed mindset. A little insider trading and corporate fraud is justified by claiming that everyone does it, that it's the invisible hand at work: everyone acts in their own narrow self-interest and, magically, society is better off.

But Adam Smith also wrote *The Theory of Moral Sentiments*, where he clearly states that we are connected to each other via strong social and emotional sentiments. Smith situated our own individualistic tendencies in a larger, more complete human frame, allowing for people to act in the interest of "their own care" or of selfish passions, which include social passions (e.g., empathy) and unsocial passions such as anger.[8] Evolutionary biologists also see human society in more complex terms, and they note that we survive largely through cooperation and living in groups.

Frans de Waal, a primatologist, conducts research on primates and the prevalence of reciprocity and fairness in animal societies. Rather than framing humans and primates as selfish, de Waal poses the question in his research, "Do primates have empathy in the sense that they are sensitive to the emotional states of others? Do they have a sense of fairness? How do they cooperate and when do they cooperate?"[9] De Waal's team recorded chimpanzees grooming each other in the morning. After a few hours, when it came time to share food, the chimps that groomed each other in the morning had a better chance of getting food from those same chimps in the afternoon. Thus, de Waal surmises that getting along in a group is critical to survival:

> I think it's absolutely essential for their life. Why would you live in a group? Because group life is better for you than solitary life. And if you live in a group and you do things together—like chimpanzees. They hunt together. They defend their territory together. And they warn each other against predators. So if you live in a group, you have to do each other favors. Otherwise, there's no point in living in a group.[10]

The chimpanzees' obligations to the group went beyond simple reciprocity. In one research group, an older female could barely walk. Younger females would gather water for her or help her climb obstacles to be with others. The favors could not be returned. Through their actions, these younger chimpanzees illustrated empathy and the need to practice a norm necessary for the benefit of the group as a whole.[11] De Waal's research matches Adam Smith's writings on social passions in that any society, even that of chimpanzees, is built at least partially on a concept of fairness. Similar research done on human infants reinforces Smith's societal view.

Rather than being based purely on selfish actions, human societies encourage individuals to work with others in a community, and they reinforce the norms of that community so that the group as a whole survives. With this lens, businesses that try to go it alone look shortsighted. It should be noted that two firms that did not survive the 2008 crash were Lehman Brothers and Bear Stearns, and many referenced their selfish behavior back in 1997 when there was a decision to be made about which businesses to save in 2008.

HOW WE TALK ABOUT BUSINESS'S ROLE IN SOCIETY MATTERS

How we frame the role of business in society matters a great deal, and there is actually a lot of variance in business press and management literature. When Facebook acts as an island, by merely putting out technology without any consideration for how the technology is embedded in existing institutions, it creates untenable situations and receives backlash. For example, Facebook partnered with Cambridge Analytica, a voter profile company, and gave them access to the data of fifty million Facebook users as well as that of their friends. This then enabled Cambridge Analytica to build psychographic profiles of those users for later targeting with political advertisements around Brexit, and for specific campaigns such as those of Ted Cruz (R-TX Senator) and Donald Trump in 2016.[12]

When, on the other hand, Facebook is made aware of how their technology interacts within existing power structures and reinforces unethical behavior, Facebook works to improve the relationship between their technology and stakeholders. Consider Facebook's recent response to criticism about how they govern their technology: "We didn't take a broad enough view of our responsibility, and that was a big mistake," and, "I think the mistake we made is viewing our responsibility as just building tools, rather than viewing our whole responsibility as making sure those tools were used for good."[13] When Facebook was shown how their technology was used to facilitate cyberbullying, they worked with researchers to design a system to identify and silence harassers. While not perfect, Facebook actively sought to understand their role within institutions and how they could better existing relationships.

Those who value individualism see themselves as having a lower obligation to others in their social network. In contrast, those who perceive the self as interdependent with others endorse collectivist values more than individualist values, perceive a higher degree of social obligations, and behave more like de Waal's chimps![14] Sometimes Facebook acts very much in its own self-interest, and other times it notes, "We need to take a more active view in policing the ecosystem and watching and looking out and making sure that all the members in our community are using these tools in a way that's going to be good and healthy."[15]

It turns out that how we teach economics may reaffirm the individualistic story. Researchers compared the values prioritized by economics students to those prioritized by students in other social science fields. Economics students placed more value on individualism, including such end goals as achievement, hedonism, and power. But this initial study included a self-selection bias: economics students could be more individualistic before taking the economics class, and the more individualistic person may be driven to *choose* economics. So the authors compared students at the beginning of their studies and then again towards the end, in both economics and non-economics majors. The researchers found that students generally became more cooperative with others as they moved towards graduation, but the trend towards cooperation was absent for economics majors. The researchers then surveyed students at the beginning and end of three courses: two economics courses (one taught by a neo-classical economist and one taught by a professor of economic development) and one course in astronomy. The researchers compared the proportion of each class, then reported how students would behave in a situation that required cooperation and honesty. The neo-economics class fared the worst, with the highest proportion (30 percent) of students reporting that they would behave in less cooperative and honest ways, and the astronomy class fared the best (10 percent).[16]

There is hope, however. The individualistic narrative is constructed by the way we talk about business and ourselves, and changing that narrative impacts behavior. Researchers were able to change people's focus on individualism versus interdependence merely by having respondents *think* about collectivist pronouns. Respondents were primed by being asked to circle "we" pronouns as opposed to "they" in a story; circling only "we" pronouns facilitated respondents to produce more socially embedded self-descriptions.[17]

The way we talk about our position within and relationship with society is powerful, and simply using different pronouns (we versus I) can overcome cultural differences. Researchers repeated the priming experiment in two cultures: one individualistic (United States) and one collectivistic (Hong Kong). The priming made the respondents switch cultures. In other words, when left to their own devices, U.S. respondents acted individualistically, and without any priming the respondents from Hong Kong were more inclined toward collectivism. However, respondents from the United States, which chronically encourages independent self-construal, endorsed more relationship- and group-enhancing goals when primed with "we" exercises that nurtured interdependence. In contrast, participants from Hong Kong, a culture that encourages interdependent self-construal, endorsed more individualistic goals when primed with independent pronouns ("I").[18] So, merely priming individuals with the language of interdependence in the U.S. sample appeared to shift values to reflect more inter-dependence goals.

This finding explains the results of the study of economics students: how we talk about individualism versus interdependence can influence the way people then prioritize values. These findings should also show the importance of the narrative leaders tell about themselves, their managers, and their firms. The more leaders talk about "we," the more people will start thinking about themselves in a socially embedded manner. Firms that believe and act as if they are embedded in a network of interdependent institutions and stakeholders succeed. We see this in the example of Facebook, where the strategies pursued in the name of Facebook-as-an-island end up being modified (sometimes much later) in the name of Facebook-as-embedded-in-institutions. We also saw this in the decline of certain banks that chose to serve their own interests in 1997 and thus did not survive the 2008 crisis.

SOCIETY IS IMPORTANT TO ALL BUSINESSES: SOCIETAL ISSUES, PARTNERSHIPS, AND INSTITUTIONAL FAILURE

Stories of poor relationships between a business and society can overwhelm the front page of our newspapers, whereas examples of businesses taking care of the institutions in their locality go under-reported. For every Walmart, who for years did not pay close attention to its communities, there is a Costco being criticized for spending *too much* attention on stakeholders rather than shareholders (for example, paying their employees well). Consider Madewell Jeans, a business making and selling jeans with a mind to performing a positive role in society, as evidenced in their Do Well program.[19] When customers buy a pair of jeans, Madewell takes donated old pairs of jeans and recycles them for housing insulation. Madewell also offers a human rights campaign, and has partnered with the Surfrider Foundation to protect coastlines and beaches, as well as invest in water-saving initiatives, since the process of making jeans uses a lot of water. In this manner, and in ways that directly offset their jeans-manufacturing business, Madewell works to positively engage with society.

Similarly, Airbnb, the peer-to-peer online marketplace for temporary housing, has started a program to match living spaces with people displaced due to natural disasters (e.g., hurricanes), medical needs, or social upheaval. The program, called Open Homes, allows current and new Airbnb hosts to offer their home to temporarily displaced people.[20] Airbnb provides background screens of hosts, reimbursements for property damage, guest verification, and support. Inspiration for the program came when hosts in New York offered temporary housing after Hurricane Sandy hit the United States in 2012. Then in 2017, Airbnb officially launched the Open Homes initiative by offering free housing for refugees through their hosts. Airbnb also works with organizations such as International Rescue Committee, which specializes in displaced people (refugees and evacuees), and leverages their core competency to make a positive impact.

Russell Ackoff, one of the pioneers of this theory that corporations should work toward the benefit of stakeholders, would often tell the story of a non-U.S. company realizing that the government had a much bigger influence on its future than did more traditional stakeholders such as customers and suppliers. Despite this fact, they spent virtually no resources on understanding the nuances of government, nor on developing strategies to create value.

The difference in how a business works within or against societal institutions may be informed by their view of their own role in society. Researchers have examined what drives individuals to contribute to rather than exploit the common good. In studies, individuals are asked to decide how much to give to a common resource (common good) versus how much to take for themselves (common dilemma). While the scenario is structured the same—in both cases, the individual would need to give up an immediate gain for themselves for the good of the collective—the framing impacts how the individual acts. We know from research that individuals who must decide how much to *give* to a common resource are less likely to give up their resources when their social identity is low. In other words, the introduction of a collective identity increased an individual's willingness to sacrifice immediate personal gain.[21] The key is the presence of a collective identity within a smaller group: individuals who identify with a small group are more apt to work to make the collective better by contributing to the public good.[22] In the case of Airbnb, the firm acts as a member of its community, seeking to act for the community's benefit and solve its problems. In other words, individuals who see themselves as part of a smaller community or network of institutions are more likely to act with the collective interest in mind, particularly when the mindset is that everyone has some obligation to the community.

Here, again, traditionally trained economics students do not fare well. Researchers have also examined whether economics graduate students would behave in more of a self-interested manner than undergraduate or high school students (they would).[23] In a common dilemma experiment, economics students contributed an average of only 20 percent of their endowments to the public account, significantly less than the

49 percent average for students of all other subjects.[24] Possibly more interesting than the percentage who gave were the students' responses when asked about their decisions. Noneconomics students gave coherent responses to questions about the fairness of their decisions to contribute, whereas "More than one-third of the economists either refused to answer the question regarding what is fair or gave very complex uncodeable responses."[25] Some people trained in economics did not even have the vocabulary to talk about giving!

This phenomenon could explain why members of an organization such as Bitcoin behave differently from members of Airbnb. Both are part of a new business model where an organization facilitates peer-to-peer transactions. Where Airbnb matches hosts and guests for a place to stay, Bitcoin offers participants a mechanism to trade digital currency. Yet Bitcoin does not have a strong culture or purpose to guide participants. Individuals are expected to trade solely in their self-interest. Not surprisingly, members of Bitcoin have begun purposefully situating themselves in rural communities to take advantage of cheaper energy prices as the company "mines" its digital currency in once-abandoned aluminum plants.[26]

A second level illustrates not only how companies are connected with society, but also how they partner with institutions to improve their community. For example, Lyft, a ride-sharing company that provides a platform to match drivers with passengers, partnered with local institutions to combat drunk driving. In the DC area, Lyft partnered with WRAP and SoberRides to offer discounted or free rides on major drinking holidays such as Halloween, St. Patrick's Day, and the Fourth of July. Lyft also works with Budweiser for discounted rides at any time, as well as with universities such as University of Texas at Austin and University of South Carolina to offer rides to students within a defined area.

Similar to Airbnb and Madewell, these companies use their business model to partner with other institutions to address societal problems. CVS partnered with Goodwill to train unemployed veterans to be pharmacy technicians in Baltimore.[27] This included building a mock CVS pharmacy on the Goodwill premises. Trainees entered a sixteen-week training course with the goal of passing the state's pharmacy technician certification exam. CVS also provides training specifically for veterans in and around Fort Bragg, North Carolina.

These types of partnerships are a form of cooperation rather than competition. Economists research why people work to cooperate versus compete under different conditions. Those values we mentioned before—universalism and benevolence as opposed to power and hedonism—predicted respondents' tendencies to contribute to a partner in an experiment. A charity game was used to measure whether respondents would contribute under competitive conditions. Researchers found that contributions to a mock charity correlated positively with whether participants valued benevolence over so-called "power values." Moreover, when the participant was reminded of their values, the impact of those values was stronger, and participants explained their choices in terms of values that were (a) important to them and (b) relevant to the situation.[28] This could explain why some companies seek to partner with societal institutions and others maintain a more competitive stance.

Researchers have also found that when given the chance to have a free ride, or enjoy the benefits of a community without contributing, individuals that prioritize interdependent values rather than independent/power values contribute more. To test for cooperation and partnerships, participants in an experiment are assigned to one of three groups of forty people. Each group must build a pot of money based on contributions from its members. The group with the most in the pool receives the money from all three pools—regardless of whether each individual contributed.[29] Certain individuals could then enjoy the winnings without ever contributing. Not surprisingly, given the previous research, the researchers found that contributing to the group correlated positively with benevolence and negatively with power values.

In another experiment, respondents were placed into high-benevolence, high-power, and mixed groups. Overall, individuals in the high-benevolence group were twice as likely to contribute (and in greater amounts!) than participants emphasizing power values. Rendering participants' value orientation salient increased the percentage and the amount contributed by participants in the high-benevolence group, but did not significantly change the contribution of participants emphasizing power.

Much is made about companies such as Volkswagen, who created a computer program to trick the societal institutions tasked with checking their emissions. However, less discussed are those companies engaging in partnerships for the good of society, such as 3M partnering with the Michigan Department of Transportation to modernize a major interstate in order to be able to test the first connected vehicle infrastructure on a large scale and improve safety.[30] Or consider Uber's partnership with the city of Pittsburgh to pilot driverless cars and invest in the city.[31] Or, there is Bit Source that launched a startup in Kentucky to teach coal miners to code computer software.[32] Co-owners Lynn Parish and Rusty Justice repurposed an old bottling plant in order to take out-of-work miners in Appalachia and offer them new skills. Mined Minds in Pennsylvania offers a similar opportunity.[33]

To be clear, not all partnerships with institutions are the right thing to do. Some companies may be partnering in order to take *more* from the common good rather than contribute to it. Some businesses partner with governments to track down welfare recipients,[34] develop algorithms that are neither open nor fair to sentence defendants,[35] partner with public schools to harvest student data,[36] or help police prioritize who they target with a predictive crime program (think *Minority Report*).[37]

And yet we still have companies such as Facebook, Twitter, Microsoft, and YouTube, which formed the Global Internet Forum to Counter Terrorism, an initiative to combat terrorists utilizing their sites.[38] The partnership is focused on how the companies can work to stem the spread of violent extremism on their platforms, a problem they all have in common. The research shows that such partnerships are not an aberration; viewing businesses as contributing members of a community makes them more likely to address important local issues.

Many new companies that we have referred to in this book take their relationships with society one step further and set business goals centered on solving an institutional failure or taking on an important societal issue such as poverty, inequality, or global warming. These companies *exist*, at least in part, to address problems that the old narrative tells us are the purview of the government, not business.

In many ways, Callisto exemplifies this business model. Sexual assault is normally the concern of law enforcement, and societal institutions should address the issue of making sure sexual assault victims feel safe in coming forward. Callisto, which initially was established in university communities, is a software company whose product allows victims to report their assault into an information vault without disclosing the incident to authorities until the victim is ready. The victim is notified if there is a match for the perpetrator, or even just a similar incident in the same location. At that time, the victim can decide whether to report the assault to the authorities. Callisto received additional funding and is looking to expand to new communities grappling with sexual harassment and assault.[39]

Similarly, Roshni Rides is a carpooling platform in Pakistan that connects female commuters to a network of nearby riders and dependable drivers. Their goal is to create brighter lives, one ride at a time, and the platform's mission is to "empower women in Pakistan through transportation regardless of their socioeconomic class."[40]

Rather than waiting for institutions to step in to empower disenfranchised individuals, many firms are creating business models that target institutional failure and focus on a mission larger than mere profits. Consider Chanderiyaan, which was formed to bring digital connectivity to the handloom industry in Chanderi in north-central India.[41] This e-commerce portal showcases Chanderi weaving and empowers the Chanderi weavers' community by allowing its members to sell garments directly to the consumer, thus bypassing "the hefty network of master weavers."[42]

The idea is that when we see a societal wrong, it is natural to try to fix it—if we see ourselves as part of the same group. For Madewell, Callisto, Lyft, and Airbnb, the companies act more like individuals who see ourselves as embedded in societal institutions and multi-person networks.

We also see many businesses becoming active advocates against societal problems. For example, Apple pulled out of Indiana after the state legislature and governor passed anti-LGBTQ legislation. Nike supported Colin Kaepernick in the midst of a conversation about kneeling during the national anthem.[43] IBM, American Airlines, PayPal, and Apple spoke up against anti-LGBTQ bills in North Carolina,[44] and many tech companies such as Twitter, Netflix, Google, and Apple spoke out against the attempted repeal of DACA.[45] For our initial example of Salesforce, the company decided to pull out of Indiana after the passing of anti-LGBTQ legislation that the company saw as putting their employees at risk of discrimination. Once the legislation was softened, the company continued to invest in Indiana.[46]

Patagonia exemplifies this activism and refers to itself as "The Activist Company."[47] Patagonia recently decided to donate their $10 million corporate tax cut to environmental protection groups. Patagonia CEO Rose Marcario thought the 2017 tax cuts were "irresponsible" and the politicians' response to climate change "woefully inadequate."[48] Patagonia also helps their employees and customers become socially active by giving employees time off for voting and launching Patagonia Action Works, a program that connects activists with causes.[49]

BUSINESS IS EMBEDDED IN THE PHYSICAL WORLD: SOCIETAL ISSUES, PARTNERSHIPS, AND INSTITUTIONAL FAILURE AGAIN

The impact of pollution on the environment and its role in climate change comes into sharper focus with each passing year. And business has navigated its role in the physical world in an evolving manner. Business has followed a typical cycle of responses to the environmental movement: manipulation, denial, avoidance, compromise, acquiescence, and then going beyond compliance.[50] In the early environmental movement, business saw scientific studies and environmental NGOs as fringe groups without much legitimacy. For example, in the early 1970s, chemical companies showed little concern with the growing evidence of the dangers of CFCs.[51] Steel companies had to be sued before they complied with the Environmental Protection Agency (EPA), as many businesses considered the agency to be illegitimate.[52] This initial disregard for environmental concerns mirrored the U.S. tobacco industry's tactics to evade regulation by the FDA.[53]

Today we see a range of ways business is embedded in the physical world that parallel the examples above. First, we have examples of businesses that are working to live in a mutually beneficial relationship with their community, who have aimed to refrain from polluting or harming the environment. McDonald's attempts to source their food products in such a way that minimizes the impact on ecosystems and biodiversity; the company also focuses on farming viability and economic stability.[54] Additionally, McDonald's aims to have 100 percent of its packaging sourced from recycled or certified sources by 2020. McDonald's also minimizes the life cycle impact of food and packaging by reducing food and packaging waste, thus protecting resources and conserving forests. We also see more sustainable solutions from firms across industries. Nike has focused on shrinking its environmental footprint by introducing ColorDry, and it dyes shirts with recycled CO_2 rather than water.[55] Similarly, Target is developing an eco-clothing line and has focused on responsible sourcing by working with vendors to make them more transparent.[56]

Second, businesses partner with nonprofit organizations to focus on environmental impact. For example, the apparel industry is a major consumer of electricity and contributor to greenhouse gas emissions.[57] To achieve its goal of using 100 percent renewable energy by 2025, Nike collaborated with MIT Climate CoLab to hold a competition called Materials Matter to quantify the environmental impact of different material choices for garments. In the competition, one team created an app where designers can estimate the impact of their material choices on the climate, fitting into a movement of sustainable clothing. And Patagonia was a founding member of the Textile Exchange, in partnership with other like-minded companies, in a move to better understand the social and environmental benefits of environmentally conscious textiles.

The food industry has seen companies partnering up on environmental issues as well. For example, McDonald's, which initially created a lot of packaging and solid waste, has partnered with the Environmental Defense Fund to focus on waste reduction and minimization of its environmental footprint. The result was a reduction in materials used, a greater commitment to recycling, and increased composting. The company also switched from its polystyrene packaging to more easily recycled paper. Starbucks partners with organizations such as the Association of Postconsumer Plastic Recyclers, Business for Social Responsibility, and Conservation International, specifically to collaborate on environmental impact and ethical sourcing. This is in addition to their work to pursue more environmentally friendly packaging, retail, and energy strategies.[58]

Finally, we have examples of companies taking on institutional failures in the area of the environment. For example, the Vietnamese company Fargreen was formed to handle the waste product of the rice industry. Vietnam is a large exporter of rice, but rice production creates a problematic byproduct: rice straw. The straw is usually burned, which causes pollution. The founder of Fargreen, Trang Tran, instead developed a business model where the straw is used to grow gourmet mushrooms, which can be sold. The leftover is then used as bio-fertilizer for rice crops, thus fixing the pollution problem and offering a sustainable additional income for rice farmers.

Patagonia has also become active in taking on institutional failures. The company joined a coalition of Native American and grassroots groups to challenge President Trump's attempt to reduce the coverage of national parks and monuments in Utah.

For Patagonia, such a step was a natural outgrowth of their work maintaining national parks by partnering with "tribes, climbers, canyoneers, trail runners and anglers."[59] Immediately after Trump's decision to cut the lands, Patagonia put a statement on their website saying, "The President Stole Your Land."[60]

■ ■ ■

In this chapter, we have examined the myth from the old story that business is set in some mythical free-market land where it exists as an island, selfishness is a virtue, ordinary rules don't apply because competition is perfect, and the invisible hand is everywhere. The new story updates this assumption to show how business has always been firmly embedded in society. Business is reliant on societal norms, infrastructure, and laws as it works with societal organizations to solve key problems. Research shows that talking about this new story actually impacts how we see ourselves in relation to our community and leads us to act more in keeping with our instincts to survive in a group. Patagonia's selflessness with regards to environmental action and political activism no longer looks out of place in business literature: individuals and businesses who see themselves as embedded in a community look to that same community for issues to address and prospective partners. However, the assumption of the selfish individual still looms over our very idea of business, as well as our understanding of human society as a whole. We now move to examine how the new story of business will replace this outdated idea.

Chapter 6

HUMANITY AND ECONOMICS

PEOPLE ARE COMPLICATED

Key Ideas

- Human beings have evolved to be both self-interested and other-regarding.
- Beyond pure rationality, people make decisions in accordance with their emotions, values, and identities.
- Framing people as nothing more than economic maximizers misses what drives humans and groups.
- People and organizations are morally complex, and as such improvement matters more than perfection.

A HUMAN STORY

Maria Almeida[1] is a bright, hard-working, and talented undergraduate student majoring in computer science and business.

She's at the top of her class at a well-regarded university, and as she finishes her senior year, she's been researching companies where she might want to work. She has multiple job offers, given her outstanding resume and infectious energy. Her first offer is from a well-known technology company that has a reputation for its innovative products and cutthroat work culture. Employees are generally overworked and unhappy, and turnover at the company after a few years is quite high. Maria has another offer at a tech company that is known to be a great place to work. The company cares about its impact on stakeholders, as well as the environment and society at large, and employees generally stay for much of their careers. The decision is difficult for Maria because the second company pays 25 percent less than the first, even after she negotiated her prospective salary up. Which job should she choose?

What we think Maria should do, and what we ourselves might do in this situation, is dependent on what we think about human beings, what motivates them, and what they need to be happy. If Maria is predominately financially motivated, she might take the first offer because it pays significantly more and could set her up for a more lucrative jump later in her career. If, however, Maria cares about other things such as relationships, happiness, values, and her impact on others, then she might seriously consider the second offer even if the salary is lower. Research shows that millennials are more likely to sacrifice a higher paycheck in exchange for a better quality of life and work that they believe in. The current estimates show that millennials are willing to take up to 15 percent of a cut in pay to work at a company that aligns with their values.[2]

Organizations also make assumptions about human beings and what motivates them. Increasingly, organizations are finding ways to revise parts of the traditional story in favor of more accurate and useful assumptions. For example, 1) instead of assuming that people are either self-interested or altruistic, companies are adopting a view, based on evolutionary psychology, that human beings are both self-interested and other-regarding, depending on the context; 2) instead of segmenting people as being either rational utility maximizers or irrational, we argue that people have a variety of tools for coping with the world, such as emotions, values, and relationships, that are differentially useful in different situations; finally, 3) instead of the assumption that people and organizations are either all good or all bad, a more useful description is that people and organizations cannot be neatly classified into such morally absolute categories as heroes/villains or saints/sinners. Moral complexity, and the idea that the same person or organization can act in admirable ways in one situation but can also make serious mistakes in another, is being taken more seriously. In this chapter, we will walk through each of these ideas in more detail and provide examples of companies that are embracing these assumptions to create more value.

PEOPLE ARE SELF-INTERESTED
AND OTHER-REGARDING

One of the most critical assumptions we make about ourselves and others is whether we are more self-interested or more altruistic.[3] Some scholars of business maintain that people act primarily in their own self-interest, even when they claim to be appealing to values.[4] This view makes the motivations behind altruism a puzzle. This view matters because what we think others will do shapes our behavior and sets our expectations of which kinds of behaviors merit praise or blame. If we think others are more likely to be self-interested, we are more likely to act that way as well.

Evolutionary psychologists have begun to piece together a much more complex view of human morality. Rather than being a puzzle that has to be explained, in their view, morality becomes a core evolutionary advantage because it fosters the cooperation and coordination that sets human beings apart from other great apes. Evolutionary psychologist Michael Tomasello argues that humans became "ultra-social" because of their hunting tactics.[5]

Humans and chimpanzees have different strategies for collecting food. Chimpanzees gather fruit individually, whereas evidence suggests that humans have been working together to hunt large game as early as four hundred thousand years ago. By working together, humans increased their odds of eating and therefore of surviving. Chimpanzees, on the other hand, have to be extensively trained to cooperate. Lab experiments have attempted to train chimpanzees to pull together on a rope that is connected to a board with food. However, they show no natural ability to work together or divide their labor to accomplish a task. While chimps, bonobos, and orangutans have shown that they are capable of many activities once thought to be uniquely human, such as tool-making, empathy, friendships, and discerning the goals of others, they cannot work together in complex ways.

Tomasello and his colleagues argue that collaboration to gather food was just the beginning. Working together allowed human beings to see themselves in relation to others as part of a group. Tomasello calls this shared intentionality, the idea that two minds are paying attention to the same thing and working toward the same goals. Shared intentionality is also a basis for morality, which psychologists classify in two broad ways. The first is emotional: feeling concern for others, usually those we interact with closely. The second is more systematic, including concerns for justice and fairness that extend beyond our kin and close partners. Shared intentionality makes both feeling concern for others as well as concern for justice and fairness possible, because both require understanding a situation from the perspective of another person.

Tomasello and other evolutionary psychologists show that human beings have multiple systems of morality. We care about 1) our own survival, 2) specific partners such as friends and family that we need for key resources, and 3) abstract moral principles embodied in systems, processes, and rules. Indeed, human infants start at a younger age than previously thought to care about the people close to them, and to be motivated to help them without direct benefit to themselves. At five or six years old, most children develop a more abstract morality and are willing to punish or reward others not because they personally know them, but because they have violated or met specific moral standards. So if evolutionary psychology is telling us that people are neither purely selfish nor purely altruistic, and that they have multiple systems that regulate behavior, how do we know when one system will prevail over others?

For many years, psychologists believed that there were fixed personality traits and that people had individual differences that made them more or less self-interested or altruistic.[6] Most of this research was conducted using self-reported surveys, and we all know that people can say one thing on a survey and do another in real life. Consequently, there was very little reliability across those surveys.

Starting in the 1960s, social psychologists like Stanley Milgram[7] argued that human behavior was less a product of unchanging and fixed personality traits than of human beings reacting to the details of specific situations. This view, called situationalism, has shaped social psychology ever since. Milgram became famous for a research paradigm called Obedience to Authority, where he showed that people, when caught up in a difficult situation, were likely to act in ways they did not predict. Milgram's work has been replicated in many countries by dozens of scholars, and has provided consistent results over several replications.

For example, as demonstrated by his experiment at Yale University, people will often obey the orders of an authority figure, even if those orders go against their own conscience. In this class of experiments, participants came into the lab and were assigned the role of the "teacher" in what they thought was an experiment on memory and learning. The teacher's job was to teach word pairs to the "learner," an actor who was in on the experiment. When the learner got a word pair wrong, the subject was to administer what they thought was an electric shock. The learner, whom the subject could hear but not see, would then respond by crying out in pain and begging to be let out. Of course, when asked if they would shock another human being past their willingness to continue, most people would say, of course, they wouldn't do so. But Milgram showed that a majority of people, over 50 percent in some conditions, continued to administer electric shocks when urged to do so by the experiment's authority figure, up to 450 volts and past the point at which they feared for the learner's safety. Milgram's argument was that most people were conditioned to obey an authority figure, and that their values and beliefs are secondary to navigating such a situation.

There are a variety of studies in social psychology that show how a particular situation can impact human behavior.[8] For example, when there's a mirror in the room, people cheat less at a variety of tasks.[9] Conversely, when the room is dark, people are more likely to cheat.[10] Factors such as group identity, incentives, and perception of costs and benefits impact the likelihood of behaving in certain ways.[11] In contrast, personality-based research seeking to show a correlation between certain personality traits and certain behaviors has not been as successful in explaining behavior.

When we are put in situations where others are acting selfishly, we are more likely to act selfishly; when we're put in situations where we see others acting selflessly, we are more likely to do the same. People choose how to interpret a situation, and that in turn influences their decision to act more selfishly, altruistically, or in the interest of the group. For example, one social experiment had participants play a prisoner's dilemma game, where they chose either to cooperate with others or help themselves, and their ultimate reward was dependent on what their partner did. If the game was framed as "the business game," people acted to benefit themselves more than if the game was called "the community game," in which case more people cooperated.[12]

Companies are building on these insights and finding ways to leverage what we know from psychology about human behavior to help create organizations that reward and recognize both our self-regarding and other-regarding nature. For example, at Google there's a complex system of rewards and recognition that builds on our multiple moral systems.[13] This includes a peer bonus system where any employee can nominate a co-worker to be the recipient of a small bonus, usually around $175. Managers or supervisors can give a spot bonus of anywhere between $500 and $3,000, which is used as a tool to recognize and reward special behavior. By showing appreciation for employees that go above and beyond their normal duties, Google motivates its staff to take care of others and themselves.

What's more, Google found that money was not always the best motivator for its employees. They began using other rewards to recognize outstanding work: fancy dinners, new tech gadgets, and fully paid vacations, for example. Google also devised an internal tool, called "gThanks," in which any employee can recognize and publicize on a group feed the good work or excellent performance of another employee. This peer-to-peer recognition program is more effective than simply praising a colleague one-on-one.[14] Google's theory of human behavior is more complicated than rational utility maximization, working off of the premise that "simple public recognition is one of the most effective and most underutilized management tools."[15]

PEOPLE HAVE A BROAD TOOLKIT FOR MAKING SENSE OF THE WORLD

In addition to being both self- and other-regarding, human beings have a complex toolkit for navigating the world. In business, we tend to adopt the economics perspective and assume that rationality is the only, or at least the most useful, tool, and we downplay the importance of other tools such as emotions, values, and identity. Let's explore how each works.

EMOTION

In a classic experiment, researchers have shown that we're a lot more emotional in our decision-making than we would like to believe.[16] Think about two hypothetical job offers, each offering a three-year contract. In the first job, you would make $90,000 the first year, $100,000 the second year, and $110,000 in the final year. In a second job, you'd make $120,000 in your first year, $110,000 in your second year, and $100,000 in the final year. Most people would take the first job rather than the second because, even though option two has more money overall, having your paycheck reduced *feels* bad. Similarly, research on confirmation bias repeatedly shows people are not objective consumers of information; we're more likely to believe information that makes us feel good and confirms our existing beliefs than information that disconfirms our existing beliefs and therefore makes us feel anxious or uncertain.

Emotions can be very functional—they help us navigate the world and motivate our actions. In familiar situations, our emotions and intuitions can be a good guide for action, but in more novel situations, our emotions might lead us astray. Reasoning can also lead us to make suboptimal decisions in specific circumstances. Chen-bo Zhong, a management scholar at the Rotman School of Management in Toronto, shows that when directed to *think* versus *feel*, people donate less to charity and are less likely to help others.[17] Additionally, as people are taught that self-interest is rational, they act in more self-interested ways. Some of our research has shown that the amount of exposure to economics in undergraduate studies is a strong predictor of how much a person believes that morality is worth the effort: if people are self-interested, then it takes work to be other-regarding. These participants are also more likely to cheat when given a chance.[18]

VALUES

Just like emotions, values also have an important role in our decision-making. Let's assume that someone was trying to make a decision as methodically and carefully as possible by modeling the consequences of their choice. We can return to the example of Maria and what job she should take. Maria could try to identify how her two job options vary and compare them; she would have to rank different criteria such as salary, location, and culture. Those weights are not objective but come from her values—what she cares about and what kind of career she wants to have. Values influence our choices in profound and sometimes less obvious ways.

In a now-classic study, Joshua Knobe offers a first scenario:

> The vice-president of a company went to the chairman of
> the board and said, "We are thinking of starting a new pro-
> gram. It will help us increase profits, but it will also harm the
> environment." The chairman of the board answered, "I don't
> care at all about harming the environment. I just want to
> make as much profit as I can. Let's start the new program."
> They started the program. Sure enough, the environment
> was harmed.[19]

Researchers asked participants whether the chairman
had intentionally harmed the environment. A majority of
participants—82 percent—replied yes. In a separate situation,
participants reviewed the same scenario but with the word
"help" substituted for the word "harm":

> The vice-president of a company went to the chairman of the
> board and said, "We are thinking of starting a new program. It
> will help us increase profits, but it will also help the environ-
> ment." The chairman of the board answered, "I don't care at all
> about helping the environment. I just want to make as much
> profit as I can. Let's start the new program." They started the
> program. Sure enough, the environment was helped.[20]

Surprisingly, when asked if the chairman had intentionally helped the environment, the results reversed, and only
23 percent of participants said he did. Similar results show

that negative outcomes make it easier to blame someone, but positive outcomes do not necessarily earn the scapegoat equal amounts of praise. Our values-based assessment of helping and harming influences whether we think the chairman acted intentionally or not.

Similarly, researchers have found that people value much more than financial outcomes. Of course, we need a certain level of financial security. Research has shown that after $75,000 a year, money has diminishing returns on happiness.[21] Other factors that influence happiness include increased levels of autonomy, competence, and relatedness. Autonomy is about freedom, choice, and the ability to make one's own decisions. Competence is about improving one's ability, feeling like one has the skills to address a challenge. Relatedness is about feeling like a part of a group that shares the same purpose. Researchers have shown that, whether at work or at home, human thriving is dependent on these three psychological needs, and that people vary in how they satisfy those needs.

We might like to assume that customers act rationally, but this often leads to our being blindsided when they respond against our expectations. Coca-Cola tried an experiment in which they changed the price of a Coke in vending machines based on the outside temperature.[22] So during hot weather, a cool drink became more expensive than during cool weather. From an economic theory perspective this makes perfect sense because price is related to supply and demand—but Coke had to pull the machines off the market because customers, who accused the company of "gouging," didn't use logic based on the precepts of a free-market economy to evaluate their choices, but the values they held—specifically fairness.[23] It may not be perfectly rational from Coca-Cola's standpoint, but when people's values are offended they can react strongly and swiftly.

IDENTITY

Another important driver of human behavior is identity. Human beings create and enact their own identities. Identity is about answering the question, "Who am I?" In doing so, people draw on the multitude of social groups that provide a basis for different identities. Therefore, one specific individual can have a variety of different identities. For example, Victoria is a manager, a mother, a painter, a daughter, a Latina, a community leader, and a faithful churchgoer, and each of these identities is differentially available for both Victoria and others to make sense of and judge her actions in specific situations.

By trying to manage their identities, individuals seek validation from their colleagues and peers. An individual's identities are "confirmed" when others recognize and support those identities. According to Laurie P. Milton and James D. Westphal, "Identity confirmation is a psychological state that exists when an individual's social environment is consistent with his or her self-identities."[24] It signals a perceived congruence between how a group member defines him- or herself and how other group members define that person. Individuals are thus motivated to find social support, especially for those identities that are central to their self-concept and salient in a particular context.

Individuals work to have their identities confirmed by society at large. In a classic study, scholars found that people who held a negative view of themselves were more likely to spend time with others who also held a negative view of them, rather than seeking out a more positive peer group.[25]

Co-workers may confirm each other's identities behaviorally, by assigning tasks to individuals that are consistent with those individuals' self-identities, or verbally, by talking about someone in a manner consistent with their self-identity. For example, if Victoria defines herself as hardworking, intelligent, and compassionate and her co-workers also define her that way, both parties have a congruent set of expectations about Victoria. People may notice that others do not see the same level of complexity about themselves when their self-identities and expectations about what they can do are not supported in their social context.

Identity confirmation has been shown to have several positive effects on individuals and groups. At the individual level, identity confirmation is associated with positive psychological states such as security, well-being, and the desire to create predictable relationships.[26]

Organizations are relying on these psychological insights to create more compelling work environments. Recent Gallup surveys show that 50–70 percent of the workforce is disengaged at work—that means a lot of value is left on the table.[27] Companies could seize a key competitive advantage if they were able to unlock the passion and intrinsic motivation of their workforce. Experiments such as 20 percent time—where employees can use 20 percent of their time at work to explore ideas that interest them—encourage autonomy. At Google, many key applications, such as Google Maps and Google Translate, were the fruition of someone's 20 percent time.

A large body of research in organizational behavior and psychology is converging on the idea that embracing the complexity of human motivations, among them increased autonomy, competence, and relatedness, can have significant business advantages.[28]

In a 2002 Gallup meta-analysis of almost eight thousand business units in thirty-six companies, researchers found there was a strong relationship between employee satisfaction and engagement and business unit outcomes such as customer satisfaction, productivity, profitability, turnover, and the number of accidents or mistakes. The more engaged and satisfied the employees, the higher the productivity, satisfaction, and profitability, and the lower the turnover and the number of accidents. The study authors say, "In summary, the strongest effects were found relative to employee turnover, customer satisfaction–loyalty, and safety."[29] And they found that "business units in the top quartile employee engagement measured 1 to 4 percentage points higher in profitability."[30] This is consistent with the research from London Business School finance professor Alex Edmans, who finds that companies that are consistently on Fortune's Best Places to Work list financially outperform their competitors by somewhere between 3 percent and 5 percent.

Since the 1950s, business schools have been led by economists who oversimplify human behavior when trying to understand large-scale economic phenomena. These oversimplifications lead to assumptions that may be useful when predicting GDP but are less useful when actually leading a team and building a culture that produces enduring economic results. By understanding how people use emotions, values, identity, and intrinsic motivation, leaders can embrace the new story of business and unlock human potential to build organizations that flourish.

PEOPLE AND ORGANIZATIONS ARE MORALLY COMPLEX

People and organizations can act in morally positive ways in one context and negative ways in another. The same person can donate to charity and also be rude to a cashier. The same company can take really good care of its employees and have a poor record when it comes to the environment. Despite this complexity, most people try to make summary judgments that simplify the individuals' motives and behaviors. Research shows that there is a bias towards negative information—negative information is more easily remembered, and we overvalue it when it comes to assessing an individual's or organization's character. This makes sense because we've evolved to avoid harm and risk. The idea that if someone does something wrong, they are a bad person to be avoided can motivate you to limit your exposure to that person. This instinct can be counterproductive if you have to work with that person, or if your judgment and subsequent treatment of this person end up reinforcing their bad behavior.

Additionally, people tend to make judgments about groups that may not be true for all members of the group. For example, someone might believe that companies only care about profits and talk about purpose to disguise their greed. While that may be true in some cases, there are also companies that care deeply about purpose and make serious investments to benefit their stakeholders. The generalization that all businesses only care about profits throws the baby out with the bathwater.

No person is always a saint or always a sinner. Nor is an organization always a hero or always a villain. The point of this is that it is best to reserve moral judgment for a specific *action* rather than to summarize a person or organization. We want to be careful before we label a person, organization, or institution. If people are complicated and we care about improving behavior, then we need to reframe the question from "are you a good person or bad person?" to "how can you improve and become better?" In an increasingly complex world, a single mistake can damage an individual's or organization's reputation, and we need ways of salvaging our credibility and our ability to act after a mistake.

Starbucks takes good care of its employees through tuition programs, increased training, and better pay. In 2015, Starbucks launched the campaign #RaceTogether as a response to racial violence throughout the United States.[31] The idea was that customers coming to a Starbucks could have a conversation about race with their Starbucks barista to promote awareness of important issues. The #RaceTogether logo was put on coffee cups in an effort to call attention to racial justice in the country. Despite noble intentions, Starbucks and its CEO Howard Schultz were lambasted for this initiative because people did not want to have deep conversations about race with their Starbucks barista, and Starbucks employees were ill-equipped to actually have these conversations with customers in a productive way. To question whether Starbucks is a good company or a bad company distracts from what's important about this example, which is how Starbucks should have shaped the campaign to make it more effective. To do that well, they would have needed to train their employees to engage with customers in a way that would be most effective for each.

Examples such as Starbucks coming under fire for their misguided attempt at entering the conversation about race are increasingly likely because organizations are being monitored from multiple angles. Research by the brand-consulting firm APCO that administers the Champion Brands survey shows that there is a type of consumer they call a "stakebroker."[32] Stakebrokers are not your traditional opinion leaders or influencers who read the news and talk to people about their opinions; they are highly engaged individuals who look at companies from a 360-degree perspective. What makes this audience unique is not just that they are more informed and active than standard consumers, but that they engage with companies from the perspectives of *all* traditional audiences and their respective interests simultaneously (consumers, community members, environmentalists, policy influencers, employees, and investors). These stakebrokers communicate with multiple audiences to influence their perception of a particular brand, and to help other stakeholders see how the value they obtain from the company is generated.

In a world where people and organizations are complicated, stakeholder companies need to build skills of relationship repair and resilience. Organizations need a way of apologizing for unintended harms, and of committing to fixing the situation. When stakeholders see a wrongdoer show credible signs of remorse for mistakes, and take tangible actions towards repairing the problem and preventing similar things from happening in the future, they are more likely to forgive, and trust in the company can actually increase. As an example, FedEx makes a promise to deliver their customers' packages on time. Yet, in the face of unpredictable weather, that can be hard to do. Therefore, FedEx flies twenty-five to thirty airplanes at 60 percent capacity each night, so that they can be rerouted to help in areas where severe weather might otherwise prevent them from making deliveries on time. By planning for failure and building systems to help them be resilient, companies like FedEx can live up to their values in an increasingly complex world.[33]

■ ■ ■

In this chapter, we've examined three related myths from the old story: that people are self-interested, rational, and simple. The new story of business updates these assumptions to embrace how people have multiple moral systems that help them attend to the self and others; how the human brain uses tools such as emotions, values, identity, and intrinsic motivation to cope with the world; and finally that people are complicated and will make mistakes. Organizations are using these insights to improve how they treat their employees, customers, and other stakeholders.

As we return to Maria, we see that for her and a growing number of millennials, the paycheck is an important but insufficient criterion for selecting a job. To attract top talent, organizations must understand human psychology and how to build organizations and systems that lead to human flourishing.

People want to belong to an organization that does something that matters. They want a chance to develop their autonomy, relatedness, and competence, and to become who they want to be. To create environments that bring out the best in us means revising our assumptions about what makes people tick.

Chapter 7

BUSINESS AND ETHICS

BUSINESS AND ETHICS MUST BE INTEGRATED INTO HOLISTIC BUSINESS MODELS

Key Ideas

- Business decisions involve ethical considerations.
- Many of our incomplete narratives about business rely on separating ethics from business.
- We have to integrate our economic interests with our broader human interests, and our models of business need to reflect such integration.
- Research shows that when business is intentional about addressing ethical considerations, it can create positive outcomes and increased trust with stakeholders.
- Companies around the world are making tangible investments in responsible operations.

CarMax is a used-car retailer whose core values include doing the right thing, putting people first, winning together, and going for greatness. Within the context of their first value listed, their primary value statement is, "We value integrity above all else." These values fit in well with their specified commitments to social responsibility, diversity, and having a positive impact on society. When it comes to their commitment to diversity, they are not just referring to their employees but to other stakeholders as well, to "ensure every associate, applicant, customer, vendor, and shareholder is treated equitably, and we respect the attributes they offer." CarMax also created the CarMax Foundation that focuses on community engagement programs.[1]

CarMax's "Code of Business Conduct" is a resource that clarifies for employees the business's principle of working with integrity. Bill Nash, president and CEO of CarMax, states in his opening message, "As a CarMax Associate, there will be times when you may confront difficult ethical situations and have a choice to make. Our Code provides tools and resources to help guide you and to ensure that we continue to conduct our business with integrity."[2]

CarMax focuses on four aspects of social responsibility: communities, environment, work life, and customers.[3] They engage in various social responsibility initiatives within each of these categories. For environmental impact, they strive to maximize recycling, minimize waste, conserve water, and much more. To assess their progress in this area, they release a "Greenhouse Gas 'Net-Zero' Feasibility Report," which uses a standardized protocol developed by the World Business Council for Sustainable Development and the World Resources Institute.[4]

CarMax isn't perfect, and it is highly likely that, like all the companies mentioned in this book, they can find ways to better live up to their purpose and values. Nonetheless, we can see from these statements that they are attempting to integrate their sense of purpose, their ethical values, and their everyday practices. This integration of traditional "business" concerns with "ethics" concerns is a hallmark of these new models of business.

THE NEED FOR BUSINESS AND ETHICS TO BE INTEGRATED

Vocabularies are important. If we tell students that business and ethics don't mix, or take the joke about "business ethics is an oxymoron" seriously, then they will apply that mindset in the real world. Social science is self-fulfilling in this sense. It is thus crucial to figure out a new vocabulary that lets us see business as an institution of hope while actively improving it.

The grain of truth here is that we have, in fact, separated business and ethics in our incomplete business models. Sometimes ethics is simply added on later to the core business model under the rubric of corporate social responsibility, or seen as a side constraint on what is permissible behavior.

Indeed, one of the main pillars of this book is that in the traditional narrative of business, business and ethics are separate elements. A hallmark of the new story of business is that companies are beginning to treat business and ethics as complementary. According to Conscious Capitalism, business is founded on a moral basis of lifting people out of poverty and increasing the wealth of everyone involved. According to the people concerned with ESG or Impact Investing, the social effects of a business, which are clearly an ethical matter, can also radically affect the traditional measures of the bottom line. Even those who follow Michael Porter's Shared Value approach see the interconnection between economic value and societal value.[5]

Most people want to do business with companies that are committed to acting ethically. No company is perfect, but the idea that most businesspeople act unethically most of the time is not very useful. Our experience with thousands of businesspeople and their stakeholders is that ethics matters to them. For every scandal-ridden company like Enron, there are thousands of companies with folks just trying to do the right thing. We shouldn't let the worst business actors represent the whole institution.

Since the 2008 global financial crisis, there has been increasing pressure for companies to be more transparent and explicit about their ethics. One initiative based on the new model of business, JUST Capital, surveys the public and ranks every company of a certain size based on what they are doing with respect to key societal and ethical issues. In this new atmosphere of public pressure for business accountability, one of the best ways for executives to respond is to understand how their ethics are connected or could be connected to the company's underlying business model.

There is no better example than SC Johnson, a manufacturer of household chemical and cleaning supplies. Their motto is "A family company at work for a better world." This ethos has been with SC Johnson for several generations. Herbert F. Johnson Sr., the son and successor to the company's founder, once stated, "The goodwill of people is the only enduring thing in any business. It is the sole substance. The rest is shadow."[6] This philosophy is manifested to this day by SC Johnson's commitment to publicly sharing their environmental and social impact with integrated annual Sustainability Reports, which they have been releasing for over twenty-five years.[7]

To demonstrate that they are serious about transparency and accountability in this area, they have developed what they call their "GreenlistTM." This initiative is "SC Johnson's peer-reviewed, science-based program that evaluates the impact on human health and the environment for every ingredient we use." They have used it to inform their product development since 2001 in an effort to continuously improve their operations. The current CEO and chairman, Fisk Johnson, includes a message at the beginning of the 2017 Sustainability Report that builds off of Johnson Sr.'s 1927 quote: "What matters most: The trust you put in our company and our products, and our commitment to live up to that trust, each and every day."[8]

In 1976, SC Johnson's leader, Sam Johnson, developed the company's business principles into a formal document titled "This We Believe," which became their guide for how to conduct business. SC Johnson uses this principle-driven approach when considering the key stakeholders, which are segmented into five distinct groups: employees, consumers and users, the general public, neighbors and hosts, and the world community. Fisk Johnson sums up their business ethics: "This We Believe calls on us to act with integrity, respect people, make responsible choices and pursue growth so we can keep doing good in the world."[9]

If we understand business as being about how humans create value for and trade with each other, then as a practice it is as old as human society itself. We have specialized our labor and cooperated to create value since living in hunter-gatherer tribes. The idea that business is inextricable from ethics should be a settled question by now. Because the old narrative insists that business is about narrowly defined self-interest, especially reducible to "money," it puts the question of the ethics of business front and center.

When we say that business and ethics are integrated, we mean that business choices have ethical implications—after all, what business decision does not 1) impact how others make sense of our virtues and values; 2) involve social norms, rules, and laws; and 3) generate harm and benefit to different stakeholder groups? Doing business means interacting with ethics—this does not mean that by default business decisions are morally good. Business leaders must wrestle with moral questions and figure out what a "good" decision is in the context of themselves and their stakeholders.

Therefore, there are important ethical questions in business, just as there are in any other human endeavor, but the overarching question of whether or not value creation and trade is in itself an ethical practice has by and large been answered. It is fundamental to who we are as human beings, and it has brought about an enormous amount of good. Sometimes bad actors have taken advantage of most people's tendency to be trusting and cooperative, and much harm has been done in the name of business. The new models of business and our five fundamental ideas behind these new models all build explicitly on the idea that business and ethics must always be combined.

What we need is a capability to think through ethics issues when there are competing moral claims. We need tools and skills to integrate business and ethics when conflicts arise. In short, we need to learn to have better conversations about how business and ethics can be integrated.

BUSINESS MUST HAVE SOCIETAL LEGITIMACY

Businesses must have societal legitimacy if they are to continue to operate effectively in society. Many new-model companies have interpreted "societal legitimacy" in a way that focuses on building their communities. The well-documented business-ethics scandals over the past half-century have proven that societal legitimacy is easy to lose. One need only think about Enron or Volkswagen. While the number of companies that are untouched by scandal far outweighs the few that are, business as a legitimate institution in society has lost its high standing. Becoming a community or society builder is increasingly important. Significant research by Sybille Sachs and her colleagues spells out the conditions that are necessary if companies are to maintain a "license to operate" from society.[10]

American Express, a financial services corporation, is interested in helping build strong communities, and it focuses its charitable endeavors in leadership development, preserving historic places, and strengthening communities.[11] American Express aims to strengthen communities by providing disaster relief support and grant funding for nonprofit organizations. They created a program called "Serve2Gether," which fosters employee volunteering and makes it easier for employees to connect with local nonprofits in their area of interest as well as promote these causes with their colleagues. Additionally, American Express provides micro-grants to employees' preferred nonprofits, as well as a free financial consulting program that nonprofits can avail of over the course of multiple months.[12]

American Express hopes to develop leaders who will help solve complex social problems, and they have spent over $70 million since 2008 to train more than seventy thousand of these "social purpose leaders." To achieve this, they founded the American Express Leadership Academy, a global program that has been hosted in eleven countries, with training both online and in person. American Express also offers ongoing support for these leaders with alumni programs and an online platform where everyone can share their stories after the official training is completed.[13]

3M, a large conglomerate with businesses from worker safety to consumer goods, takes a different approach to societal legitimacy by focusing on building sustainability into its business model, including how it deals with its communities. Current CEO Mike Roman has a prominent statement on 3M's About Us webpage: "At 3M, we use science to improve lives and help solve the world's toughest challenges. We remain focused on executing our plans, and continuing to deliver exceptional value for our customers and premium returns for our shareholders." On this same webpage, they list four categories: Who We Are, How We Innovate, Corporate Responsibility, and Business Practices. Each category is displayed at the same level, which indicates that they are of equal importance.[14]

In the dropdown menu for Corporate Responsibility, 3M delves into their sustainability philosophy. Here we see them mention, "Our commitment to Sustainability drives our purpose-driven innovation that improves every life, and we are always trying to do more." To this end, they include their 2018 Sustainability Report that one can download to review their progress metrics and sustainability initiatives.[15]

In addition to sustainability as an independent concept, 3M has been actively involved in community engagement. They have "3Mgives" initiatives, which they label their "social investment arm" that helps them to "maximize the company's community impact and support a culture of service among our people." Their annual 3Mgives report contains the many social impact initiatives they are currently engaged in within their stakeholder communities.[16]

In terms of its Business Practices, 3M emphasizes their ethics and compliance practices, code of conduct, and commitments. They also have an independent ethics and compliance team that reports to a separate audit committee within the 3M Board of Directors. They state, "Our employees know they don't have to compromise their ethics to do business. Our customers know we are a company they can trust. At 3M, we are committed to do the right thing every day."[17] These practices are put in place to build trust with stakeholders. Or as Roman articulates, "Great and enduring companies are driven by purpose, and built on a foundation of trust – trust from our customers, employees, partners, shareholders, and communities. At 3M, we cannot break that trust – ever."[18]

Alibaba, a Chinese e-commerce and technology company, is also serious about transparent accountability to the public. In a push to engender public trust, in 2018 they released their first ESG report to bring light to their operations and impact. In a preface for the ESG report, Executive Chairman Jack Ma states, "We believe that a profitable and prosperous business can only be achieved and sustained by solving large-scale societal problems." They believe focusing on their human capital (i.e., employees) will enhance their social impact, and they have many programs to foster a culture built on employee satisfaction, inclusiveness, and professional development.

With this foundation in nurturing human capital, Alibaba can have a significant positive societal impact in areas their business touches.[19] Through their Lakeside Modou Foundation, Alibaba created a platform focused on enabling women entrepreneurs to start and grow their businesses in rural areas of China. This platform both creates jobs in underdeveloped areas and provides a potentially transformative opportunity for women and their families.

Alibaba is also leveraging artificial intelligence (AI) technology and partnering with cities to reduce traffic problems in congested areas. Alibaba provides the technology, and the cities own the transportation data collected. The platform, called "City Brain," allows municipalities to optimize their transportation infrastructure (e.g., traffic lights) to alleviate congestion and reduce pollution. Alibaba also hopes they can develop it into an open, cloud-based platform that can spur innovation by allowing businesses and research institutions to leverage the power of this interconnected system.[20]

WHAT RESEARCH TELLS US

There is a growing body of research that supports integrating ethical concerns with other business concerns. First, research by sociologist Brian Uzzi shows that entrepreneurial organizations benefit from strong relationships with stakeholders, including suppliers.[21] In studying organizations in the garment industry, Uzzi found that when relationships are strong, suppliers can provide novel information that allows entrepreneurs to take advantage of new trends and become more competitive. When there were any problematic issues or misunderstandings, mutual trust led to cooperative problem-solving. Whereas when a relationship was purely transactional, problems were more likely to result in costly legal negotiations that destroyed value. Uzzi argues that there is an optimal level of embeddedness in a relationship that allows each party to benefit from it while avoiding costs such as barriers to change.

A second body of research shows that a company that engages in ethical behaviors leads to increased trust by others. In the context of negotiations, scholars Kong, Dirks, and Ferrin examined thirty-eight different negotiation studies and found that as trust in the other party increased, negotiators were more likely to use integrative behaviors, or behaviors that share information and increase vulnerability, whereas less trust was related to more distributive behaviors or acts to claim more value.[22] As integrative behaviors increased, both individual and joint outcomes improved, as did satisfaction with the negotiation. Ethical behavior increased trust, which in turn helped generate better negotiation outcomes.

Conversely, when people are blind to the ethical impacts of their actions, researchers call that moral disengagement. When people are morally disengaged, they are less likely to take the perspective of others and more likely to perpetrate unethical behaviors.[23] Therefore, by integrating business and ethics, and highlighting the moral nature of business, leaders can reduce the likelihood that members of their organization will conduct unethical acts, lose the trust of their stakeholders, and destroy value for the organization.

■ ■ ■

The myth that business and ethics are mutually exclusive tells an incomplete story; worse, the story leads to bad outcomes by focusing too narrowly on profits, ignoring the interests of key stakeholders, pretending that business is an island, and treating people in business as selfish wealth maximizers. Instead, we are constantly integrating our economic interests with our broader human interests—and business is no different. Our best models are those that incorporate such integration. There are many ways to integrate business and ethics. There is no one "right" way.

As this global revolution in how we understand the new story of business proceeds, we need to take a step back and ask what can executives who have been laboring in the grip of the old story do to make their companies more up to date for the challenges of the twenty-first century.

Chapter 8

REALIZING THE NEW STORY

Key Ideas

- Many companies need to focus on employee engagement and building trust with stakeholders.
- There are useful tools that can help businesses reenergize their purpose, build trust with stakeholders, integrate with society, engage employees, and integrate business and ethics.
- The time for change is now, and businesses need to assume a leadership role.

NEW YORK LIFE AND THE NEW STORY OF BUSINESS

New York Life, founded in 1845, is a mutual insurance company, meaning its policyholders are also its owners or shareholders. Many mutual companies are run just like shareholder value-oriented companies in the old story of business, focusing primarily on ROE and other financial metrics. New York Life is different in that it embodies each of the five key ideas of the new story of business.[1]

First of all, the company itself is purpose-driven, focusing on "providing long-term financial security for its policyholders." Of course, this still means it has to be profitable. In the words of CEO and Chairman Ted Mathas, "While ROE is irrelevant, that doesn't mean we don't care where every dollar is invested. But, ROE is not our purpose." Mathas further states, "of course we have to be profitable, but profits are a means to an end. The end is the long-term financial security of our policyholders." And New York Life has been outrageously successful as a purpose-driven company. Its stock has paid a dividend every year since 1854, it has over $1 trillion worth of life insurance under management, and it is routinely rated the number one life insurance company. Mathas believes that a strong commitment to purpose is the key to financial strength: "Purpose, when you really mean it, drives companies to be more disciplined than just focusing on profits or ROE."

Second, New York Life understands that it must create value for all of its stakeholders. While customers are of prime importance, so too are employees, local communities, as well as agents, regulators, and other key stakeholders. One way to put it is that New York Life extends the responsibility of their purpose to "the larger communities where we work and live through our commitment to a diverse workforce, an ethical culture, deep community engagement, and a sustainable planet."[2] In addition, Mathas believes that the company needs to think about future policyholders, employees, and others. And the best way to accomplish this is to see a company as enmeshed in a set of relationships that exist over time, rather than a discrete set of transactions for the short term. According to Mathas, such relational thinking allows people to "grow the pie" since relationships are not zero-sum games. Mathas understands his role as being a steward for the company, and to ensure it lives on to benefit society.

Third, New York Life is committed to being involved in society. It has devoted itself, donating time and money, to finding solutions to a number of societal issues. For instance, it has worked with educational institutions, focusing on transitions with respect to middle school students. The New York Life Foundation has also supported research on grief for parents at Columbia University, partnering with the Alliance for Strong Families on a program called "Building Resilience in the Face of Disaster" to address the long-term effects for communities that have been hit with tragic events.

Fourth, New York Life's Ted Mathas has a complicated understanding of what makes people tick. He says that people are different, and the only way the company can thrive is to acknowledge, understand, and celebrate these differences. Mathas believes that one of the key components of the new story of business is the recognition that people need to understand their own narrative, as well as be a part of something bigger than themselves. How people see purpose, stakeholders, societal relationships, and ethics is really just a shorthand for what is important about an individual's and a business's own narrative. Individuals who embrace their own and their business's narrative can have individual accountability for what they do, while taking "collective pride" in the accomplishments of the group as a whole.

A culture of trust is the glue that holds New York Life together, according to Mathas. This is especially important in today's society, where trust is under fire from a number of directions. In a letter to employees, Mathas writes, "Trust is not something we can ever take for granted. It must be earned and re-earned each day. Our good name is put to the test in every interaction with customers, prospects, suppliers, community leaders, public officials, and even each other."

Finally, Mathas understands that business and ethics have to be integrated into everything that New York Life does. He wants his employees to make the decisions that they make personally, eschewing the language of, "It's just business, it's not personal." Mathas says, "It's always personal. Companies don't make decisions; people do. Individuals, as well as companies, need to take responsibility for their decisions, or ethics can never be integrated with business." In a letter to employees, Mathas writes, "Our core value of Integrity is central to all facets of New York Life's business. Everything we do is dependent on people believing that we will never take chances with their future and trusting that we will always live up to the promises we make."

Like Salesforce, Blackrock, Whole Foods, Patagonia, CarMax, and all the other companies mentioned in this book, the picture we have painted of New York Life might seem too good to be true. However, at some point, we have to stop and ask ourselves why we have so much skepticism about businesses that seem to make our lives better. One obvious answer is, again, the saints-and-sinners problem. No business, just like no person, is perfect, and every organization is capable of improving. The old story of business holds us in its grip if we let it. However, the existence of these "new-story businesses" (some of which are very old) offers a different path for the future. In the following sections, we will outline some tools for improvement that we have observed these new-story businesses employing.

RECOVERING AND RE-ENERGIZING PURPOSE: ASKING TOUGH QUESTIONS

As more and more conversation is taking place about the power of purpose-driven organizations, many businesses have begun to recover and re-energize their purpose where appropriate. For example, Company Y, a large public company in a traditional industrial sector, noticed that its purpose statement didn't differentiate it from any other company in the industry. Yet, the newly appointed CEO felt that the company treated its people better, was more customer- and stakeholder-oriented, took its societal obligations seriously, and prioritized putting ethics and business together. He believed that there was something there that the company was simply ignoring, so he undertook a project outlining a series of conversations around questions like:

- Who are we?
- What do we stand for?
- What does society expect from us?

- What do we want others to say about us?
- How can we get young talent to join us?
- What do we need to change?

These conversations went on for six months and resulted in a much-revised statement of purpose that was both aspirational and unique to the company. The next set of conversations dealt with creating a platform for change, for, as we have seen, if a company's purpose is not reflected in its set of systems and processes, then it is likely to be regarded as empty words. A key moment during one of these conversations was when the CEO asked his team whether anyone had ever pushed for a change, given the old statement. No one raised their hand, cementing the idea that the old purpose statement wasn't actually very inspirational.

Asking these tough-purpose questions, such as "if we do this, is it in line with what we say we stand for?" is a critical skill that organizations need be constantly exercising. The CEO of an Enron competitor once said that it was difficult coming into the office every day and having people tell you how stupid you were for not doing the off-books balance sheet entities that were the ultimate undoing of Enron. "But," he said, "We just didn't see how doing that added any value to our customers." Similarly, the CEO of a bank, talking about the subprime crisis, said, "We weren't hurt much by this since we didn't see how lending money to our customers that they couldn't afford to pay back, did anyone any good." In both of these cases the purpose question was the company's priority, which ultimately resulted in greater value created for both the company and stakeholders.[3]

It is also important for potential investors to ask these questions. As Wall Street moves towards taking ESG impacts into account, investors and their advisors need to be savvier in figuring out how to assess the societal effects of companies before they invest.

UNLOCKING STAKEHOLDER VALUE

Most businesses pay some attention to stakeholders. Indeed, how could they not, since customers, suppliers, employees, financiers, and society as a whole are all critical for a company's success? However, the main flaw in many companies' relationships with their stakeholders is that each stakeholder is considered independently and in isolation.

Most businesses have complex ways of measuring how they are faring with customers, or with employees, and certainly with financiers. What the new story of business tells us is that these stakeholders are interdependent. Creating value for one stakeholder automatically affects how value is created with other stakeholders, and understanding and leveraging this interdependence is one of the keys to success. Walmart pioneered supply-chain management, which in its most simple form, is simply connecting suppliers with employees and customers. Information technology at the point of sale fed data back to suppliers, so that operations could be more simply designed. Similarly, the Container Store integrated one of its suppliers with its warehouse, attached to corporate headquarters, as they sought to give the best possible customer service.

Stakeholder integration is key to unlocking potential value from the set of stakeholder relationships that make up a business. We need to ask some critical questions and develop conversations that lead to policies and practices around these questions. For instance:

- How does creating value for customers affect the value we create for other stakeholders (and ask this question for each stakeholder)?
- How are we engaging with each stakeholder? Do we know how each stakeholder wants to engage with us?
- How is our purpose connected to how we engage our stakeholders?
- Are our stakeholders trying to make our business better and more effective?
- Where are we making trade-offs among stakeholders, and how can they be avoided?
- What capabilities (know-hows) do we need to engage with multiple stakeholders?
- What partnerships do we need with stakeholders?

Having an ongoing conversation around questions like these can unlock a great deal of value, and it can lead to innovative, non-trade-off thinking. The questions are simple but the answers are not, and it takes a commitment to continuous engagement with stakeholders to create real answers. Ultimately, "stakeholder value" will come to replace the business world's preoccupation with "shareholder value" and "financial value." This transition is likely to go on for some time, until we achieve new and better methods of truly understanding the value created for stakeholders—and this includes shareholders.

Unilever has spent the past few years rethinking their purpose and unlocking stakeholder value, and they have come to the conclusion that success is built on purpose. As Alan Jope, CEO of Unilever, stated, "It is not about putting purpose ahead of profits, it is purpose that drives profits."[4] Unilever's purpose—"make sustainable living commonplace"—inspired innovation in both its production and business models, e.g., improving purposeful brands' packaging, sourcing, and waste management. The company now has twenty-six purposeful, sustainable living brands, including Dove, Lipton, Ben & Jerry's, and Hellmann's. As Unilever's website says, "We developed our 'sustainable living' brands, which have a clear purpose relating to social or environmental concern and contribute to the USLP [Unilever Sustainable Living Plan]."[5]

Unilever has pioneered the idea of unlocking stakeholder value by embracing sustainable development goals (SDG) and integrating them into corporate strategy. Stemming from the belief that the purpose of business is about serving society, Unilever has aligned its corporate vision with attaining SDGs. In 2010, the company launched the Unilever Sustainable Living Plan (USLP), a roadmap for its long-term development in a sustainable way. USLP covers all aspects of Unilever business as well as its value chain and contains concrete deliverables for achieving SDGs. As Jeff Seabright, chief sustainability officer at Unilever, mentioned, "the plan takes responsibility across the total value chain – from farm to fork and addresses external issues such as climate change, food security, deforestation, and sanitation." The results are not long in coming. Unilever has already reduced the water used in manufacturing by 44 percent per ton of production since 2008; and over half of its agricultural materials such as palm oil, paper, and tea are now sustainably sourced.

BUILDING A BETTER SOCIETY

Many years ago, a CEO of a large bank once said to us, "Why should I worry about HIV policy in Africa? We're a bank. Should I have such a policy because I'm African American, and my employees expect it? What are the limits, here?" More recently, another CEO told us that one of the most important decisions executives and boards can make is what societal issues the business must deal with, and that today there is no place to hide, no excuse for a company to sit back and do nothing. Relevant questions to ask include:

- What current and future societal issues are connected to our purpose?
- What current and future societal issues do our employees care about the most?
- What current and future societal issues affect our customers and other key stakeholders?
- What can we do with respect to the societal issues we have identified? How can we improve what is happening?

This last question may seem like a trap to executives, as they begin to focus more of their attention on societal issues. Doing so can be a complex and daunting task, and many executives have very little training on how to understand the connections between societal issues and their business models. They see that they can't solve a certain issue, and so they often say that they can't take this on. However, there is a flaw in this logic; just because a person can't singlehandedly solve World Hunger, it doesn't follow that they can't give food to a hungry person. No business can solve our most difficult social issues alone. However, they can donate money, form partnerships, and do what they can to help. Nowhere is this clearer than with regards to environmental sustainability. Here we have lots of examples of businesses that have designed processes to help.

Hershey's approach is driven by "shared goodness," which is their slogan for their sustainability approach. They articulate this as, "Today we uphold our promise with brands, business models and people making a difference in the world; being better stewards of the planet we all share; building thriving communities in the places we call home; and, perhaps most near and dear to our hearts, by nourishing the lives of children so they can learn, grow and thrive." Michele Buck, CEO, further explains this concept: "Hershey is a company that has married being purpose-driven with offering meaningful, impactful day-to-day work. The shared goodness promise is to see every day as a chance to be successful in a way that makes a positive difference."[6]

Hershey has many sustainability initiatives and charitable outreach programs. They offer financial grants to organizations in three core areas: advocating nutrition for children, supporting communities they are embedded in, and supporting businesses that wish to partner with Hershey for "win-win" solutions that prioritize other stakeholders (e.g., community, ecosystem).[7]

Hershey has also heavily invested in the sustainable farming and sourcing of cocoa, the key ingredient in many of their products. Hershey has committed to "source 100 percent certified and sustainable cocoa by 2020," and the certification process is verified by third-party auditors. Recognizing the importance of operating sustainably across the entire supply chain, Hershey also has initiatives to increase farmer incomes and improve the communities around cocoa-production areas based on their "21st Century Cocoa Sustainability Strategy." They also appreciate that improving the health of the surrounding communities improves stability and productivity, which is a win-win for their business and their stakeholders.[8]

PEOPLE, PEOPLE, PEOPLE

If there is one thing that stands at the very center of these companies mentioned that have dedicated themselves to this new model of business, it is that they all understand that business is a fully human institution. People should be at the center of every way we think about business. As we suggested earlier, business is a group of people cooperating together to solve problems that no one of them could solve alone. They do so with the full range of human abilities, emotions, identity, group affiliation, and human foibles. Every business should continuously ask itself questions like:

- Are our hiring, development, promotion, and reward systems consistent with our purpose and our claim to prioritize people?
- How do our people push back against management/executive authority? Do we value such pushback?
- Do we encourage our people to bring their whole selves to work?
- Do we encourage a sense of balance or integration in our employees' lives, and do we as executives act as role models?
- Are we creating a business that we would want our children to work in?

A number of technology companies have tried to use a variety of benefits to attract the very best people. The benefits can be clustered into the following categories:[9]

- **Basic necessities**: free food, free rides to work
- **Healthy lifestyle**: on-site fitness, free yoga, discounts to gym facilities
- **Physical and psychological health issues**: on-site medical facilities, free counseling sessions
- **Taking care of employees' dependents**: paid daycare, generous maternity/paternity leaves, bringing pets to work
- **Self-development**: stipend to travel, fully equipped music studio

- **Recreation:** free days out, ping-pong areas
- **Consumption:** product discounts

Often missing from such benefits, as attractive as they may be, is the degree to which employees actually find meaning in their work. We know that when employees see their work as meaningful, even without the free perks that some companies provide, they are both happier and more productive.

PUTTING BUSINESS AND ETHICS TOGETHER

Ethics in the twenty-first century is complicated. New technology, globalization, and difficult societal issues such as climate change often manifest themselves as ethical dilemmas that appear to be insoluble. While easy answers may not be available, we can design a framework that encourages people to ask relevant questions for making ethical decisions. Some of the questions are:

- How does this issue affect our purpose?
- Who can we involve in a conversation about what to do?
- Who is harmed by and/or benefitted from this decision?
- What relationships are most important?
- Whose rights are enabled, and whose values are realized by this decision (and whose are not)?
- What kind of person/company will I (we) become if we make this decision?

- What relationships will be strengthened or weakened by this decision?
- How will we know when it is time to change our point of view?

Putting business and ethics together works best when this approach has been built into the company's architecture from the very beginning. The Container Store (TCS) is one such company that self-identifies with the new model of conscious capitalism.[10] Its co-founder, Kip Tindell, has been one of the leaders of the new-story movement, working to unite the many strands of these new models and promote TCS's overall purpose of helping people organize their lives. Tindell has developed an extensive set of "foundational principles" to specify how TCS will realize this purpose.

Key to success is TCS's emphasis on a combination of purpose, stakeholders, building communities, focusing on the full humanity of its employees, and putting business and ethics together. TCS highlights its many stakeholder-based focuses, including putting employees first, as well as commitment to their communities and the environment, in a very basic communication of purpose: "what we stand for: an organization with heart ♥."[11] In its foundational principles, we can see how business and ethics go together. For instance, TCS believes that if you make sure consumers and stakeholders get as much value as possible, running a profitable business will take care of itself. If employees feel appreciated and find meaning in their work, the business will flourish.

■ ■ ■

We believe that we are at an inflection point in the history of business. It is high time to think broadly and creatively about how business can achieve its full potential, and how to avoid its historical weaknesses. In this book, we have outlined five key ideas or principles that we believe drive these new models of business which are emerging around the world. By focusing on the most powerful word in our language, "AND," we can take giant steps towards making the business world more responsible. In order to succeed, all of our businesses need to pay attention to: 1) Purpose and Profits; 2) Stakeholders and Shareholders; 3) Society and Markets; 4) Humanity and Economics; and 5) Business and Ethics. In addition, by thinking through this new story of business at the societal level, we can improve our institutions and help them accelerate the acceptance of the new story of business. There is much work to be done.

NOTES

1. THE NEW STORY OF BUSINESS

1. Heike Young, "20 Equality Quotes That Will Motivate You," accessed December 9, 2019, salesforce.com/blog/2017/07/20-quotes-about-equality .html.
2. "Salesforce Is Blazing a Trail Toward a Better, More Equal World," Salesforce.com, accessed April 10, 2019, https://www.salesforce.com /company/news-press/stories/2018/5/052318-a/.
3. "Take the Pledge," Salesforce.com, accessed April 10, 2019, https://www .salesforce.org/pledge-1/.
4. For a history of this debate see Duane Windsor, "Berle-Dodd Debate," in *Encyclopedia of Business Ethics and Society*, ed. Robert W. Kolb (Thousand Oaks, CA: Sage, 2008), 162–65, http://dx.doi.org/10.4135/9781412956260.n73.
5. The history of this debate is long and complicated and beyond our present scope. See Archie B. Carroll, Kenneth J. Lipartito, James E. Post, Patricia H. Werhane, and Kenneth E. Goodpaster, *Corporate Responsibility: The American Experience* (New York: Cambridge University Press, 2012).
6. "Our Commitment," Business Roundtable.org, accessed August 27, 2019, https://opportunity.businessroundtable.org/ourcommitment/.
7. Carroll et al., *Corporate Responsibility: The American Experience.*
8. William C. Frederick, *Corporation Be Good! The Story of Corporate Social Responsibility* (Indianapolis, IN: Dog Ear, 2006).

9. Archie B. Carroll, "Corporate Social Responsibility: Evolution of a Definitional Construct," *Business & Society* 38, no. 3 (1999): 268–95.

10. Dirk Matten and Andrew Crane, "Corporate Citizenship: Toward an Extended Theoretical Conceptualization," *Academy of Management Review* 30, no. 1 (2005): 166–79. A notable mark of the corporate citizenship idea is a joint statement entitled "Global Corporate Citizenship: The Leadership Challenge for CEOs and Boards" that was signed during the World Economic Forum in 2002 by CEOs of the thirty-six largest multinational companies, including Coca-Cola, Deutsche Bank, Merck, McDonald's, Philips, Renault, Siemens, and UBS; IISD, World Economic Forum Statement, International Institute for Sustainable Development (2013), accessed May 19, 2018, https://www.iisd.org/business/issues/sr_wef.aspx.

11. R. Edward Freeman, *Stakeholder Management: A Strategic Approach* (New York: Cambridge University Press, 1984/2010).

12. Michael E. Porter and Mark R. Kramer, "Creating Shared Value," *Harvard Business Review*, 89, nos. 1, 2 (2011): 62–77.

13. John Mackey and Raj Sisodia, *Conscious Capitalism: Liberating the Heroic Spirit of Business* (Boston: Harvard Business Review Press, 2013). Interested businesspeople have established about thirty conscious capitalism chapters in different cities throughout the United States and about fifteen chapters outside of the United States whose mission is to advance conscious capitalism ideas in business practices and get more conscious capitalists onboard. Currently, several hundred companies around the world identify as conscious capitalism companies; see also Conscious Capitalism Movement, accessed June 4, 2018, https://www.consciouscapitalism.org/chapters.

14. CFIC, *The Coalition for Inclusive Capitalism* (2018), accessed June 4, 2018, https://www.inc-cap.com/.

15. B Corp, The B Corp Movement. A third-party nonprofit institution certifies companies willing to live by the main ideas of the B Corp movement. Since the first nineteen B Corps were certified in 2017, more than 2,700 companies across 150 industries in 64 countries have received a B Corp certification as of May 2019. See https://bcorporation.net/, accessed May 3, 2019.

16. Richard Branson, *Screw Business as Usual: Turning Capitalism into a Force for Good* (New York: Portfolio/Penguin, 2011).

17. Scott Trubey, "Connected Capitalism Going Global," *Atlanta Business Chronicle*, April 26, 2010, last modified May 3, 2019, https://www

.bizjournals.com/atlanta/stories/2010/04/26/story7.html?b=12722544
00%5E3236431&page=1; Katherine Butler, "Former Coca-Cola CEO
Pushes 'Connected Capitalism,'" *Forbes*, April 26, 2010, last modified May 3, 2019, https://www.forbes.com/2010/04/27/coca-cola-isdell
-technology-capitalism.html#dc568c46fad9; E. Richard Brownlee, Sergiy
Dmytriyev, and Allison Elias, "Integrative Stakeholder Engagement:
Stakeholder-Oriented Partnership Between the Coca-Cola Company
and World Wildlife Fund," In *Stakeholder Engagement: Clinical Research
Cases*, ed. R. Edward Freeman, Johanna Kujala, and Sybille Sachs (Berlin:
Springer, 2017), 339–67. A good illustration of implementing the ideas
of connected capitalism into practice is the initiative launched by The
Coca-Cola Company, in which it successfully engaged its stakeholders
along the entire value chain to preserve fresh water on a global scale.

18. Shauna Carther Heyford, "Socially Responsible Mutual Funds,"
Investopedia, June 25, 2019, last modified September 12, 2019, https://
www.investopedia.com/articles/mutualfund/03/030503.asp#axzz1
Qtq4Zi2G;

Ann C. Logue, *Socially Responsible Investing for Dummies* (Hoboken,
NJ: Wiley, 2008);

Paul Sullivan, "With Impact Investing, a Focus on More Than
Returns," *New York Times*, April 23, 2010.

19. "Socially Responsible Investments Reach $30.7 Trillion," *Bloomberg News*,
April 1, 2019.

20. Annual impact investor survey 2017, Global Impact Investing Network
(GIIN), 7th edition, accessed May 19, 2019, https://web.archive.org/web
/20160902224437/https://thegiin.org/assets/GIIN_AnnualImpactInvestor
Survey_2017_Web_Final.pdf; see also "The Catholic Church Becomes
an Impact Investor," *Economist*, August 19, 2017; and Rahim Kanani,
"The State and Future of Impact Investing," Forbes.com, 2009, accessed
May 19, 2019, https://www.forbes.com/sites/rahimkanani/2012/02/23/the
-state-and-future-of-impact-investing/#5b920fd9ed48.

21. Rahim Kanani, "The State and Future of Impact Investing," Forbes.com,
February 23, 2012, https://www.forbes.com/sites/rahimkanani/2012/02/23
/the-state-and-future-of-impact-investing/#5b920fd9ed48.

22. Jacqueline Novogratz, "A Third Way to Think About Aid, filmed
June, 2009," TED video, accessed September 1, 2019, https://www.ted
.com/talks/jacqueline_novogratz_a_third_way_to_think_about_aid
/transcript?language=en.

23. Thomas L. Friedman, " 'Patient' Capital for an Africa That Can't Wait," *New York Times*, April 20, 2007; see also Jacqueline Novogratz, June 2007, TED video.

24. "What Are the Principles for Responsible Investment?" PRI Institute, accessed August 27, 2019, https://www.unpri.org/pri/what-are-the-principles-for-responsible-investment.

25. JUST Capital, Justcapital.com, accessed June 4, 2018, https://justcapital.com/.

26. "Triple Bottom Line," *Economist*, November 17, 2009; see also Devin Thorpe, "One Key to Impact Investing: Start Big," *Forbes*, May 22, 2018.

27. "The Global Reporting Initiative," Globalreporting.org, 2019, accessed May 19, 2019, https://www.globalreporting.org/information/about-gri/Pages/default.aspx.

28. United Nations, Sustainable Development Goals, Sustainable Development Goals.org, accessed May 19, 2019, https://sustainabledevelopment.un.org/?menu=1300; "Measuring Progress Towards the Sustainable Development Goals," SDG-Tracker.org, 2019, accessed May 19, 2019, https://sdg-tracker.org/.

29. Marc Benioff, *Behind the Cloud* (San Francisco: Jossey-Bass, 2009), 226–27.

30. For an explanation of the Salesforce ecosystem, see Salesforce.com, "The Salesforce Ecosystem Explained," https://www.salesforce.com/blog/2015/09/salesforce-ecosystem-explained.html.

31. R. Edward Freeman, Richard Dodd, and Jessica Pierce, *Environmentalism and the New Logic of Business* (New York: Oxford University Press, 2000).

32. "The Environment Is a Key Stakeholder," Salesforce.com, accessed September 1, 2019, https://www.salesforce.com/company/sustainability/.

33. "2019 Equal Pay Report," Salesforce.com, April 2, 2019, https://www.salesforce.com/blog/2019/04/equal-pay-update-2019.html.

34. Milton Friedman, "The Social Responsibility of Business Is to Increase Its Profits," *New York Times*, September 13, 1970.

35. "Ethical and Humane Use," Salesforce.com, accessed September 2, 2019, https://www.salesforce.com/company/ethical-and-humane-use/.

36. Dan Dammerman, "Corporate Gun Control: Salesforce.com Demands Customers Stop Selling Semi-Auto Rifles," The Truth About Guns.com, May 30, 2019. Last modified September 11, 2019, https://www.thetruthaboutguns.com/corporate-gun-control-salesforce-com-demands-customs-stop-selling-semi-auto-rifles/.

2. WHAT'S WRONG WITH THE TRADITIONAL
STORY OF BUSINESS

1. Milton Friedman, "The Social Responsibility of Business Is to Increase Its Profits," *New York Times*, September 13, 1970.
2. Michael C. Jensen and William H. Meckling, "Theory of the Firm: Managerial Behavior, Agency Costs and Ownership Structure," *Journal of Financial Economics* 3, no. 4 (1976): 305–60.
3. This section draws on R. Edward Freeman, "The New Story of Business: Towards a More Responsible Capitalism," *Business and Society Review* 122 no. 3 (2017): 449–65.
4. CBC News, "The Rise and Fall of Valeant Pharmaceutical," March 14, 2017, last modified June 21, 2019, https://www.cbc.ca/news/business /valeant-pharmaceuticals-pershing-1.4023893.
5. Steve Denning, "The Dumbest Idea in the World: Maximizing Shareholder Value," *Forbes*, November 28, 2011, last modified August 24, 2017, https://www.forbes.com/sites/stevedenning/2011/11/28/maximizing -shareholder-value-the-dumbest-idea-in-the-world/#5037docf2287.
6. Lynn Stout, *The Shareholder Myth: How Putting Shareholders First Harms Investors, Corporations, and the Public*, (San Francisco: Barrett-Kohler, 2012).
7. Hannah Roberts, "Snapchat Isn't Offering Voting Rights in Its IPO— and Potential Investors Are Furious," *Business Insider*, February 3, 2017, last modified Aug. 24, 2017, http://www.businessinsider.com/snapchat -ipo-no-voting-rights-investor-letter-2017-2.
8. Jensen and Meckling, "Theory of the Firm."
9. Stout, *Shareholder Myth*, 29.
10. Stout, *Shareholder Myth*, 29–30.
11. John Hagel, John Seely Brown, and Lang Davison, "Shift Index 2011: The Most Important Business Study—Ever?" *Forbes*, January 25, 2012, last modified August 25, 2017, https://www.forbes.com/sites/stevedenning /2012/01/25/shift-index-2011-the-most-important-business-study-ever /#4abb20743a6e.
12. Barry Ritholtz, "Where Have All the Public Companies Gone?" *Bloomberg View*, June 24, 2015, last modified August 25, 2017, https://www.bloomberg .com/view/articles/2015-06-24/where-have-all-the-publicly-traded -companies-gone-.
13. Rishi Iyengar, "This Is How Long Your Business Will Last, According to Science," *Fortune*, April 2, 2015, last modified August 25, 2017,

http://fortune.com/2015/04/02/this-is-how-long-your-business-will
-last-according-to-science/.

14. Troy Segal, "Enron Scandal: Fall of a Wall Street Darling," *Investopedia*,
May 29, 2019, last modified September 12, 2019, https://www.investopedia
.com/updates/enron-scandal-summary/.

15. Javier David, "Uber Hammered by Price Gouging Accusations During
NYC's Explosion," CNBC.com, September 18, 2016, last modified
September 12, 2019, https://www.cnbc.com/2016/09/18/uber-hammered
-by-price-gouging-accusations-during-nycs-explosion.html.

16. Adam Smith, *The Theory of Moral Sentiments*, Excercere Cerebrum,
Kindle edition, 2014, excerpted from *The Theory of Moral Sentiments*
(London, U.K.: Henry G. Bohn, 1853) 15.

3. PURPOSE AND PROFITS

1. Larry Fink, "Letter to CEOs, 2019," accessed June 21, 2019, https://www
.blackrock.com/corporate/investor-relations/larry-fink-ceo-letter.

2. Simon Mainwaring, "Purpose at Work: How Toyota Is Driving Growth,
Innovation and Impact," *Forbes*, November 13, 2018, last modified April 2,
2019, https://www.forbes.com/sites/simonmainwaring/2018/11/13/purpose
-in-action-how-toyota-is-driving-growth-innovation-and-impact/.

3. "Mobility for All | TOYOTA," Mobility for All | TOYOTA, accessed
April 2, 2019, https://www.mobilityforall.com/.

4. "Toyota USA | Environmental Protection & Sustainability Leader,"
accessed April 2, 2019, https://www.toyota.com/usa/environment.

5. "Toyota | Safety," accessed April 2, 2019, https://www.toyota.com/usa
/safety.

6. "TeenDrive365 in School," accessed April 2, 2019, http://www.teendrive
-365inschool.com/.

7. "Our Business | Barry-Wehmiller," accessed April 2, 2019, https://www
.barrywehmiller.com/our-business.

8. "Bob Chapman's Truly Human Leadership," Bob Chapman's Truly
Human Leadership—A BarryWehmiller Blog (blog), accessed April 2,
2019, https://www.trulyhumanleadership.com/?page_id=36.

9. "Meet Our Dedicated Humans | BW Leadership Institute," Barry-
Wehmiller, accessed April 2, 2019, https://www.ccoleadership.com
/about/our-team/.

10. "Ask Not What Your Employees Can Do for You; Ask What You Can Do for Your Employees," *Forbes India*, March 27, 2019, last modified April 2, 2019, http://www.forbesindia.com/article/rotman/ask-not-what-your-employees-can-do-for-you—ask-what-you-can-do-for-your-employees/52889/1.

11. "Our History," Barrywehmiller.com, accessed September 10, 2019, https://www.barrywehmiller.com/our-business/our-history.

12. "FIFCO USA: About Us," *FIFCO USA* (blog), accessed April 3, 2019, https://www.fifcousa.com/about-us/.

13. "FIFCO – Carbon Trust Zero Waste to Landfill Standard Bearer," accessed September 13, 2019, https://www.carbontrust.com/our-clients/f/fifco/.

14. "Richard 'Rick' Sharp, Co-Founder of CarMax, Dies at 67," *Washington Post*, last modified September 12, 2019, https://www.washingtonpost.com/business/richard-rick-sharp-co-founder-of-carmax-dies-at-67/2014/06/25/82794f88-fca4-11e3-932c-0a55b81f48ce_story.html.

15. The following paragraphs draw on R. Edward Freeman and Bidhan L. Parmar, "Managing for Stakeholders and the Purpose of Business," Darden Business Publishing, E-0415, and expand on ideas from R. Edward Freeman, "Managing for Stakeholders," Darden Business Publishing, E-0383, and R. Edward Freeman, Jeffrey S. Harrison, and Andrew C. Wicks, *Managing for Stakeholders* (New Haven, CT: Yale University Press, 2007).

16. Lynn Stout, *The Shareholder Myth: How Putting Shareholders First Harms Investors, Corporations, and the Public* (San Francisco: Barrett-Kohler, 2012).

17. "The HP Way," Jim Collins blog, accessed September 11, 2019, https://www.jimcollins.com/article_topics/articles/the-hp-way.html.

18. Stout, *The Shareholder Myth*.

19. Lawrence Mishel, "Economic Snapshot," Economic Policy Institute, September 24, 2013, last modified August 24, 2017, http://www.epi.org/publication/the-ceo-to-worker-compensation-ratio-in-2012-of-273/.

20. William Lazonick and Mary O'Sullivan, "Maximizing Shareholder Value: A New Ideology for Corporate Governance," *Economy and Society* 29, no. 1 (2000): 13–35.

21. GE annual report, 1971.

22. Melanie Trottman, "Top CEOs Make 373 Times the Average U.S. Worker," *Wall Street Journal*, May 13, 2015, accessed August 24, 2017, https://blogs.wsj.com/economics/2015/05/13/top-ceos-now-make-373-times-the-average-rank-and-file-worker/.

3. PURPOSE AND PROFITS

23. John Mackey and Raj Sisodia, *Conscious Capitalism: Liberating the Heroic Spirit of Business* (Boston: Harvard Business Review Press, 2013).

24. "The Rise of the Socially Responsible Business," Deloitte Global Societal Impact Survey, January 2019, accessed September 11, 2019, https://www2.deloitte.com/content/dam/Deloitte/global/Documents/About-Deloitte/deloitte-global-societal-impact-pulse-survey-report-jan-2019.pdf.

25. R. Edward Freeman and Ellen R. Auster, *Bridging the Values Gap* (San Francisco: Barrett-Kohler, 2015).

26. Mackey and Sisodia, *Conscious Capitalism*, 46. In addition, we owe this point to conversations with several former Medtronic employees.

27. A. M. Grant, "Does Intrinsic Motivation Fuel the Prosocial Fire? Motivational Synergy in Predicting Persistence, Performance, and Productivity," *Journal of Applied Psychology* 93, no. 1 (2008): 48.

28. M. S. de Luque, N. T. Washburn, D. A. Waldman, and R. J. House, "Unrequited Profit: How Stakeholder and Economic Values Relate to Subordinates' Perceptions of Leadership and Firm Performance," *Administrative Science Quarterly* 53, no. 4 (2008): 626–54.

29. Brent D. Rosso, Kathryn H. Dekas, and Amy Wrzesniewski, "On the Meaning of Work: A Theoretical Integration and Review," *Research in Organizational Behavior* 30 (2010): 91–127.

30. Claus Meyer, conversation at Copenhagen Business School in 2015.

31. Personal conversations.

32. This quotation first appears in Freeman and Auster, 42. See the interview by R. Edward Freeman with John Mackey, "What Is the Purpose of Business?" University of Virginia Darden School of Business, January 12, 2011, accessed May 15, 2019, https://www.youtube.com/watch?v=6ncsJGxkZdQ&index=2&list=PL43B5DF2B45A8B49C.

33. Harper Neidig, "Former Facebook Security Chief Says Company Needs a New CEO," *The Hill*, May 21, 2019, last modified September 1, 2019, https://thehill.com/policy/technology/444865-former-facebook-security-chief-says-company-needs-a-new-ceo.

4. STAKEHOLDERS AND SHAREHOLDERS

1. The story of the Austin flood is told in Mackey and Sisodia.

2. John Mackey and Raj Sisodia, *Conscious Capitalism: Liberating the Heroic Spirit of Business* (Boston: Harvard Business Review Press, 2013).

3. "Colgate-Palmolive – Global Household & Consumer Products," accessed April 5, 2019, https://www.colgatepalmolive.com/en-us.

4. "Colgate-Palmolive Values Caring, Sustainability & Innovation," accessed April 5, 2019, https://www.colgatepalmolive.com/en-us/core-values.

5. "Bright Smiles and Bright Futures," accessed April 5, 2019, https://www.colgatepalmolive.com/en-us/core-values/community-responsibility/bright-smiles-bright-futures.

6. "Learn About Our Purpose, Values and Culture | Interstate Batteries," accessed April 8, 2019, https://www.interstatebatteries.com/about/our-culture.

7. *Supplier Responsibility – 2019 Progress Report*, Apple, accessed April 15, 2019, https://www.apple.com/supplier-responsibility/pdf/Apple_SR_2019_Progress_Report.pdf.

8. J. K. Harter, F. L. Schmidt, and T. L. Hayes, "Business-Unit-Level Relationship Between Employee Satisfaction, Employee Engagement, and Business Outcomes: A Meta-Analysis," *Journal of Applied Psychology* 87, no. 2 (2002): 268.

9. "SAP: Corporate Social Responsibility," SAP, accessed April 1, 2019, https://www.sap.com/about/social-responsibility.html.

10. "SAP One Billion Lives (1BL) Initiative | About SAP SE," SAP, accessed April 1, 2019, https://www.sap.com/corporate/en/company/innovation/one-billion-lives.html.

11. Susan Galer, "Q&A with Adaire Fox-Martin: SAP's Purpose Is Not a Tag Line, It's Something We Live and Breathe," SAP News Center, July 18, 2018, last modified September 10, 2019, https://news.sap.com/2018/07/adaire-fox-martin-purpose-sap-one-billion-lives/.

12. "Satori Capital | What Makes Us Different / Sustainable Mindset," accessed April 17, 2019, http://www.satoricapital.com/what_makes_us_different/sustainable_mindset.

13. "Satori Capital | What We Believe / Conscious Capitalism," accessed April 17, 2019, http://www.satoricapital.com/what_we_believe/conscious_capitalism.

14. Chuck Robbins, "Building Bridges Between Hope and Possibility," blogs@Cisco-Cisco Blogs, December 2, 2018, last modified September 12, 2019, https://blogs.cisco.com/news/building-bridges-between-hope-and-possibility.

15. Housing Trust Silicon Valley, "Cisco, LinkedIn and Pure Storage Collaborate to Commit $20 Million to Housing Trust Silicon Valley's TECH Fund to Help Build Affordable Housing," November 27, 2018,

last modified April 16, 2019, https://www.prnewswire.com/news-releases
/cisco-linkedin-and-pure-storage-collaborate-to-commit-20-million
-to-housing-trust-silicon-valleys-tech-fund-to-help-build-affordable
-housing-300755642.html.

16. R. Edward Freeman, Jeffrey S. Harrison, Andrew C. Wicks, Bidhan
L. Parmar, and Simone DeColle, *Stakeholder Theory: The State of the Art*
(Cambridge, UK: Cambridge University Press, 2010).

17. Gerben S. van der Vegt, Peter Essens, Margareta Wahlström, and Gerard
George, "Managing Risk and Resilience," *Academy of Management
Journal* 58 (2015): 971–80.

18. Zachary Whitman, Joanne Stevenson, Hlekiwe Kachali, Erica Seville,
John Vargo, and Thomas Wilson, "Organisational Resilience Following
the Darfield Earthquake of 2010," *Disasters* 38, no. 1 (2014): 148–77.
Accessed September 14, 2019, https://onlinelibrary.wiley.com/doi/full
/10.1111/disa.12036?casa_token=LhuKtXj4yGsAAAAA%3A_yh
-4ClNGre1kU7DpKdRefQ-MHdp8D4A4lPivkr8U5mdsUmfY
-5jQVr8RvICBE7GFbip4ZsKfseaMimZ6; Natalia Ortiz-de-Mandojana
and Pratima Bansal, "The Long-Term Benefits of Organizational Resilience
Through Sustainable Business Practices," *Strategic Management Journal* 37,
no. 8 (2016): 1615–31. Accessed September 14, 2019, https://onlinelibrary
.wiley.com/doi/abs/10.1002/smj.2410.

19. Bill George, *Authentic Leadership* (San Francisco: Jossey-Bass, 2004),
102–4.

20. One reason economists love trade-offs is because they are fun to graph.
However, we have not empirically proven this theory.

21. Carrie Brownstein, "Whole Foods: Quality Standards and the Multi-
Stakeholder Process," Whole Foods Market, January 27, 2012, last
modified September 10, 2019, https://www.wholefoodsmarket.com/blog
/whole-story/quality-standards-and-multi-stakeholder-process.

22. "Sustainable and Impact Investing in the United States Overview, 2016,"
US/SIF Foundation, accessed August 25, 2017, http://www.ussif.org
/files/Infographics/Overview%20Infographic.pdf.

23. Alex Edmans, "28 Years of Stock Market Data Show a Link Between
Employee Satisfaction and Long-Term Value," *Harvard Business Review*,
March 24, 2016, https://hbr.org/2016/03/28-years-of-stock-market-data
-shows-a-link-between-employee-satisfaction-and-long-term-value.

24. Dominic Barton, James Manytika, Tim Koller, Robert Palter, Jonathan
Godsall, and Josh Zoffer, "Where Companies with a Long-Term

View Outperform Their Peers," McKinsey and Company, February 2017, accessed August 25, 2017, http//www.mckinsey.com/global-themes /long-term-capitalism/where-companies-with-a-long-term-view -outperform-their-peers.

25. Raj Sisodia, David Wolfe, and Jagdish N. Sheth, *Firms of Endearment: How World-Class Companies Profit from Passion and Purpose* (Upper Saddle River, NJ: Wharton School Publishing, 2014).

26. Wayne F. Cascio, "Decency Means More Than 'Always Low Prices': A Comparison of Costco to Walmart's Sam's Club," *Academy of Management Perspectives* 20, no. 3 (2006): 26–37.

27. Mary Sully de Luque, Nathan T. Washburn, David A. Waldman, and Robert J. House, "Unrequited Profit: How Stakeholder and Economic Values Relate to Subordinates' Perceptions of Leadership and Firm Performance," *Administrative Science Quarterly* 53, no. 4 (2008): 626–54; and, Bidhan L. Parmar, Adrian Keevil, and Andrew C. Wicks, "People and Profits: The Impact of Corporate Objectives on Employees' Need Satisfaction at Work," *Journal of Business Ethics* 154, no. 4 (2019): 1–21.

28. Witold J. Henisz, Sinziana Dorobantu, and Lite J. Nartey, "Spinning Gold: The Financial Returns to Stakeholder Engagement," *Strategic Management Journal* 35, no. 12 (2014): 1727–48.

5. SOCIETY AND MARKETS

1. "Sustainable Apparel Coalition," Patagonia, accessed September 13, 2019, https://www.patagonia.com/sustainable-apparel-coalition.html.

2. Dan Defrancesco, "The 'Midtown Uniform' Is Now in Peril as Patagonia Isn't Accepting New Finance Clients for Its Ubiquitous Fleece Vests," *Business Insider*, April 2, 2019, last modified September 13, 2019, https:// www.businessinsider.com/the-midtown-uniform-is-now-in-peril-as -patagonia-isnt-accepting-new-finance-clients-for-its-ubiquitous -fleece-vests-2019-4.

3. Akane Otani, "Patagonia Gives Cold Shoulder to Finance Bros Not Yet Vested," *Wall Street Journal*, April 9, 2019.

4. For the classic statement of the development of markets in an historical sense, see Fernand Braudel, *The Structures of Everyday Life: Civilization and Capitalism, 15th to 18th Century* (New York: Harper and Row, 1982).

5. These two companies did not survive the 2008 market crash, and many of CEOs recalled Fuld's and Cayne's decisions back in 1997. See Andrew

Ross Sorkin, *Too Big to Fail: The Inside Story of How Wall Street and Washington Fought to Save the Financial System—and Themselves* (New York: Penguin, 2009).

6. Roger Lowenstein, "Long-Term Capital Management: It's a Short-Term Memory," *New York Times*, September 7, 2008, https://www.nytimes .com/2008/09/07/business/worldbusiness/07iht-07ltcm.15941880.html.

7. Richard Dawkins, *The Selfish Gene* (Oxford: Oxford University Press), 3.

8. Patricia H. Werhane, "Business Ethics and the Origins of Contemporary Capitalism: Economics and Ethics in the Work of Adam Smith and Herbert Spencer," *Journal of Business Ethics* 24, no. 3 (2000): 185–98.

9. "Frans de Waal: Do Animals Have Morals?" NPR.org, accessed September 16, 2018, https://www.npr.org/templates/transcript/transcript .php?storyId=338936897.

10. Ibid.

11. Ibid.

12. Robinson Meyer, "The Cambridge Analytica Scandal, in Three Paragraphs," *Atlantic Monthly*, March 20, 2018, https://www.theatlantic .com/technology/archive/2018/03/the-cambridge-analytica-scandal -in-three-paragraphs/556046/.

13. However, we will return to Facebook as a counter-example. When Facebook did not want to moderate content in the United States and defended Holocaust deniers: John Shinal, "Mark Zuckerberg Doesn't Want to Be Your News Editor," *CNBC*, February 2, 2018, last modified September 13, 2019, https://www.cnbc.com/2018/02/02/mark-zuckerberg -doesnt-want-to-be-your-news-editor.html.

14. Wendi L. Gardner, Shira Gabriel, and Angela Y. Lee, " 'I' Value Freedom, but 'We' Value Relationships: Self-Construal Priming Mirrors Cultural Differences in Judgment," *Psychological Science* 10, no. 4 (1999): 321–26.

15. John Shinal, "Mark Zuckerberg Doesn't Want to Be Your News Editor."

16. Robert H. Frank, Thomas Gilovich, and Dennis T. Regan, "Does Studying Economics Inhibit Cooperation?" *Journal of Economic Perspectives* 7, no. 2 (1993): 159–71.

17. Marilynn B. Brewer and Wendi Gardner, "Who Is This 'We'? Levels of Collective Identity and Self Representations," *Journal of Personality and Social Psychology* 71, no. 1 (1996): 83.

18. Gardner, Gabriel, and Lee, " 'I' Value Freedom, but 'We' Value Relationships: Self-Construal Priming Mirrors Cultural Differences in Judgment."

19. Madewell website, accessed September 13, 2019, https://www
.madewell.com/on/demandware.store/Sites-madewellUS-Site/default
/Home-Show?cgid=women.

20. Airbnb website, accessed September 13, 2019, https://www.airbnb.com
/openhomes.

21. Marilynn B. Brewer and Roderick M. Kramer, "Choice Behavior in
Social Dilemmas: Effects of Social Identity, Group Size, and Decision
Framing," *Journal of Personality and Social Psychology* 50, no. 3 (1986): 543.

22. Larger groups were more self-interested and less likely to give (more
likely to take) from the common good.

23. Frank, Gilovich, and Regan, "Does Studying Economics Inhibit
Cooperation?"

24. Gerald Marwell and Ruth E. Ames, "Economists Free Ride, Does
Anyone Else?: Experiments on the Provision of Public Goods, IV,"
Journal of Public Economics 15, no. 3 (1981): 295–310.

25. Frank, Gilovich, and Regan then conducted their own field test about charitable giving and found the proportion of free riders among economists was
9.3 percent versus only 1.1 percent of other professional school respondents.

26. Patrick McGeehan, "Bitcoin Miners Flock to New York's Remote Corners,
but Get Chilly Reception," *New York Times*, September 19, 2018, https://
www.nytimes.com/2018/09/19/nyregion/bitcoin-mining-new-york
-electricity.html.

27. "Heroes2Careers Military Hiring Program," accessed September 13,
2019, https://cvshealth.com/about/diversity/heroes-to-careers-military
-hiring-program, and "Baltimore City Community College, Goodwill
Industries, and CVS Health Launch Mock Pharmacy for Specialized
Training in Baltimore," *PR Newswire*, October 10, 2018, last modified
September 13, 2019, https://www.prnewswire.com/news-releases/baltimore
-city-community-college-goodwill-industries-and-cvs-health-launch
-mock-pharmacy-for-specialized-training-300729058.html.

28. Lilach Sagiv, Noga Sverdlik, and Norbert Schwarz, "To Compete or to
Cooperate? Values' Impact on Perception and Action in Social Dilemma
Games," *European Journal of Social Psychology* 41, no. 1 (2011): 64–77.

29. Ibid.

30. The four-month construction project along I-75 added technology
such as all-weather lane markings and reflective smart tags for human
and automated drivers to see more easily, http://www.michigan.gov
/mdot/0,4616,7-151–412752–,00.html.

31. Peter High, "Why Did Uber Pilot Driverless Cars in Pittsburgh? Here's Why," *Forbes*, January 24, 2017, last modified September 12, 2019, https://www.forbes.com/sites/peterhigh/2017/01/24/why-did-uber-pilot-driverless-cars-in-pittsburgh-here-is-why/#7c6f229a43b0.

32. Adele Peters, "This Kentucky Startup Employs Former Coal Miners and Teaches Them to Code," *Fast Company*, April 18, 2016, last modified on September 12, 2019, https://www.fastcompany.com/3058929/this-kentucky-startup-employs-former-coal-miners-and-teaches-them-to-code.

33. Prachi Patel, "The Kentucky Startup That Is Teaching Coal Miners to Code," *IEEE Spectrum*, February 15, 2017, last modified September 12, 2019, https://spectrum.ieee.org/energywise/energy/fossil-fuels/the-kentucky-startup-that-is-teaching-coal-miners-to-code.

34. Kellen Browning, "Sacramento Welfare Investigators Track Drivers to Find Fraud. Privacy Group Raises Red Flags," *Sacramento Bee*, August 10, 2018, https://www.sacbee.com/news/local/article216093470.html.

35. Mitch Smith, "In Wisconsin, a Backlash Against Using Data to Foretell Defendants' Futures," *New York Times*, June 22, 2016, https://www.nytimes.com/2016/06/23/us/backlash-in-wisconsin-against-using-data-to-foretell-defendants-futures.html.

36. Natasha Singer, "For Sale: Survey Data on Millions of High School Students," *New York Times*, July 31, 2018, https://www.nytimes.com/2018/07/29/business/for-sale-survey-data-on-millions-of-high-school-students.html.

37. George Joseph, "The LAPD Has a New Surveillance Formula, Powered by Palantir," *The Appeal*, May 8, 2018, last modified September 13, 2019, https://injusticetoday.com/the-lapd-has-a-new-surveillance-formula-powered-by-palantir-1e277a95762a.

38. "Partnerships," GIFCT website, accessed September 12, 2019, https://gifct.org/partners/.

39. Lux Alptraum, "Can Callisto Transform How Silicon Valley Deals with Sexual Harassment?" *The Verge*, April 17, 2018, last modified September 12, 2019, https://www.theverge.com/2018/4/17/17247566/callisto-platform-silicon-valley-sexual-harassment.

40. Roshni Rides, accessed September 10, 2019, https://roshnirides.com.

41. "Chanderiyaan: Weaving Digital Empowerment into the Indian Handloom Industry," *William Davidson Institute* (blog), accessed September 9, 2018, https://wdi-publishing.com/product/chanderiyaan-weaving-digital-empowerment-indian-handloom-industry/.

42. "About Us," *Chanderiyaan*, accessed September 2, 2019, https://www
.chanderiyaan.net/about-us.

43. Uday Sampath, "Nike's Kaepernick Ad Spurs Spike in Sold-Out
Items," *Reuters*, September 19, 2018, last modified September 12, 2019,
https://www.reuters.com/article/us-nike-kaepernick/nikes-kaepernick
-ad-spurs-spike-in-sold-out-items-idUSKCN1LZ2G4.

44. David A. Graham, "The Business Backlash to North Carolina's LGBT
Law," *The Atlantic*, March 25, 2016, https://www.theatlantic.com/politics
/archive/2016/03/the-backlash-to-north-carolinas-lgbt-non-discrimination
-ban/475500/.

45. Joseph Hincks, "CEOs from More Than 400 Leading U.S. Companies
Urge Trump to Keep DACA," *Fortune*, September 5, 2017, https://fortune
.com/2017/09/05/daca-trump-dreamers-business-leaders/.

46. James Briggs, "Salesforce Uses Expansion to Push for LGBT Rights in
Indiana," *Indy Star*, May 5, 2017, https://indystar.com/story/money/2016
/05/06/salesforce-uses-expansion-push-lgbt-rights-indiana/84035760/.

47. "The Activist Company," Patagonia website, accessed September 13, 2019,
https://www.patagonia.com/the-activist-company.html.

48. Ryan W. Miller, "Patagonia Plans to Donate $10 Million Saved from Trump
Tax Cuts to Environmental Groups," *USA Today*, November 29, 2018,
https://usatoday.com/story/money/2018/11/28/patagonia-money-saved
-trump-tax-cut-environmental-cause/2143733002/.

49. Cara Salpini, "Patagonia Doubles Down on Sustainability," *Retail Dive*,
January 16, 2019, last modified September 13, 2019, https://www.retaildive
.com/news/patagonia-doubles-down-on-sustainability/546144/.

50. Jorge E. Rivera, *Business and Public Policy: Responses to Environmental and
Social Protection Processes* (Cambridge: Cambridge University Press, 2010).

51. Ibid., 24.

52. Press Conference, Attorney General John Mitchell, Department of
Justice, December 18, 1970, last modified September 12, 2019, https://www
.justice.gov/sites/default/files/ag/legacy/2011/08/23/12-18-1970.pdf.

53. Jorge Rivera, *Business and Public Policy*, 28.

54. "Our Food," McDonald's website, accessed September 13, 2019, https://
corporate.mcdonalds.com/corpmcd/scale-for-good/our-food.html.

55. Aparna Bansal, "Nike's Race Against Climate Change," *Harvard Business School Digital*, November 4, 2016, last modified September 12, 2019,
https://digital.hbs.edu/platform-rctom/submission/nikes-race-against
-climate-change/; "Nike Introduces First Product with ColorDry

5. SOCIETY AND MARKETS

Technology," Nike website, June 13, 2014, last modified September 13, 2019, https://news.nike.com/news/nike-introduces-first-product-with -colordry-technology.

56. "Trending: Stella McCartney, Patagonia, Target Deliver Big Wins for Ethical, Sustainable Fashion," *Sustainable Brands*, October 5, 2017, last modified September 12, 2019, https://sustainablebrands.com/read/walking -the-talk/trending-stella-mccartney-patagonia-target-deliver-big-wins -for-ethical-sustainable-fashion.

57. "MIT Climate CoLab and Nike Call for Materials Innovation to Combat Climate Change," *Nike News*, September 25, 2015, last modi- fied September 13, 2019, https://news.nike.com/news/nike-inc-and-mit -climate-colab-materials-innovation-to-combat-climate-change; Stefanie Koperniak, "MIT Climate CoLab, in Collaboration with Nike, Launches New Materials Competition," MIT Energy Initiative, October 30, 2015, last modified September 13, 2019, http://energy.mit.edu/news /mit-climate-colab-in-collaboration-with-nike-launches-new-materials -competition/; Materials Matter 2016, "Fabrics and Textiles Impact Our Climate—a Lot. How Can We Spark a Materials Revolution by Rethinking How We Value and Use Them?" Climate CoLab, accessed September 13, 2019, https://www.climatecolab.org/contests/2016/materials -matter.

58. "Environment: Pioneering Sustainable Solutions," Starbucks website, accessed September 13, 2019, https://www.starbucks.com/responsibility /environment.

59. "Hey, How's That Lawsuit Against the President Going?" The Clean- est Line, Patagonia website, April 9, 2019, last modified September 13, 2019, https://www.patagonia.com/blog/2019/04/hey-hows-that-lawsuit -against-the-president-going.

60. William Cummings, "'The President Stole Your Land,' Patagonia Home- page Says," *USA Today*, December 4, 2017, last modified September 13, 2019, https://www.usatoday.com/story/news/politics/onpolitics/2017/12 /04/anti-trump-patagonia-message/921542001/.

6. HUMANITY AND ECONOMICS

1. Maria Almeida is a composite character based on several of our students.

2. Peggie Pelosi, "Millennials Want Workplaces with Social Pur- pose. How Does Your Company Measure Up?" *Talent Economy*,

February 20, 2018, last modified September 13, 2019, https://www
.chieflearningofficer.com/2018/02/20/millennials-want-workplaces
-social-purpose-company-measure/.

3. Emily Esfahani Smith, "Is Human Morality a Product of Evolution?" *The Atlantic*, December 2, 2015, https://www.theatlantic.com/health /archive/2015/12/evolution-of-morality-social-humans-and-apes/418371/.

4. O. E. Williamson, "Opportunism and Its Critics," *Managerial and Decision Economics* 14, no. 2 (1993): 97–107.

5. Michael Tomasello, "The Ultra-Social Animal," *European Journal of Social Psychology* 44, no. 3 (2014): 187–94.

6. Walter Mischel, *Personality and Assessment* (Mahwah, NJ: Lawrence Erlbaum & Associates, 1996).

7. Stanley Milgram, "Behavioral Study of Obedience," *Journal of Abnormal and Social Psychology* 67, no. 4 (1963): 371.

8. Kenneth S. Bowers, "Situationism in Psychology: An Analysis and a Critique," *Psychological Review* 80, no. 5 (1973): 307.

9. Edward Diener and Mark Wallbom, "Effects of Self-Awareness on Antinormative Behavior," *Journal of Research in Personality* 10 no. 1 (1976): 107–11.

10. Chen-Bo Zhong, Vanessa K. Bohns, and Francesca Gino, "Good Lamps Are the Best Police: Darkness Increases Dishonesty and Self-Interested Behavior," *Psychological Science* 21 no. 3 (2010): 311–14.

11. Francesca Gino, Shahar Ayal, and Dan Ariely, "Contagion and Differentiation in Unethical Behavior: The Effect of One Bad Apple on the Barrel," *Psychological Science* 20 no. 3 (2009): 393–98.

12. Gerald C. Kane, "Which Game Are You Playing?" *MIT Sloan Management Review*, January 10, 2014, https://sloanreview.mit.edu/article /which-game-are-you-playing/.

13. Stephanie Begveni, "7 Ways to Recognize Your Employees and Save Millions of Dollars," LinkedIn Talent Blog, June 17, 2015, last modified September 12, 2019, https://business.linkedin.com/talent-solutions/blog /2015/06/9-ways-to-recognize-your-employees-and-save-millions-of -dollars.

14. Adam Kearney, "We Digitized Google's Peer Recognition," May 2, 2016, last modified on September 12, 2019, https://medium.com/@K3ARN3Y /how-google-does-peer-recognition-188446e329dd.

15. Jane Lemons, "The Best Places to Work on Planet Earth: 5 Tips to Reward and Recognize Employees Like Google," *Bucketlist* website, December 11,

2017, last modified September 13, 2019, https://bucketlistrewards.com
/employee-recognition/best-places-to-work-on-earth-tips-to-reward
-and-recognize-your-employees-like-google/.

16. Max H. Bazerman and Don A. Moore, *Judgment in Managerial Decision Making* (New York: Wiley, 1994), 226.

17. Long Wang, Chen-Bo Zhong, and J. Keith Murnighan, "The Social and Ethical Consequences of a Calculative Mindset," *Organizational Behavior and Human Decision Processes* 125 no. 1 (2014): 39–49.

18. Madeline Ong, Julia Lee, and Bidhan Parmar, "Lay Theories of Homo Economicus: How and Why Does Economics Education Make Us See Honesty as Costly?" *American Psychologist*, Under Review.

19. Joshua M. Knobe, "Intentional Action and Side Effects in Ordinary Language," *Analysis* 63 (2003): 191.

20. Ibid.

21. Belinda Luscombe, "Do We Need $75,000 a Year to Be Happy?" *Time Magazine*, September 6, 2010.

22. David Leonhardt, "Why Variable Pricing Fails at the Vending Machine," *New York Times*, June 27, 2005.

23. Ibid.

24. Laurie P. Milton and James D. Westphal, "Identity Confirmation Networks and Cooperation in Work Groups," *Academy of Management Journal* 48 no. 2 (2005): 191–212.

25. William B. Swann, Alan Stein-Seroussi, and R. Brian Giesler, "Why People Self-Verify," *Journal of Personality and Social Psychology* 62 no. 3 (1992): 392.

26. Milton and Westphal, "Identity Confirmation Networks and Cooperation in Work Groups."

27. Jim Harter, "Dismal Employee Engagement Is a Sign of Global Mismanagement," *Gallup* website, accessed September 12, 2019, https://www .gallup.com/workplace/231668/dismal-employee-engagement-sign -global-mismanagement.aspx.

28. Edward L. Deci and Richard M. Ryan, eds., *Handbook of Self-Determination Research* (Rochester, NY: University of Rochester Press, 2004).

29. James K. Harter, Frank L. Schmidt, and Theodore L. Hayes, "Business-Unit-Level Relationship Between Employee Satisfaction, Employee Engagement, and Business Outcomes: A Meta-Analysis," *Journal of Applied Psychology* 87 no. 2 (2002): 268–279, p. 274 doi:10.1037/0021 -9010.87.2.268.

30. Ibid., p. 275.

31. Sydney Ember, "Starbucks Initiative on Race Relations Draws Attacks Online," *New York Times*, March 18, 2015, https://www.nytimes.com/2015 /03/19/business/starbucks-race-together-shareholders-meeting.html.

32. "APCO Research Identifies Champion Brands, and What Makes Them," *Holmes Report*, January 27, 2013, last modified September 12, 2019, https://www.holmesreport.com/latest/article/apco-research-identifies -champion-brands-and-what-makes-them.

33. Karl E. Weick and Kathleen M. Sutcliffe, *Managing the Unexpected* (Vol. 9) (San Francisco: Jossey-Bass, 2001).

7. BUSINESS AND ETHICS

1. "CarMax Culture and Values," accessed April 10, 2019, https://www.carmax .com/about-carmax/culture-diversity.

2. *CarMax Code of Conduct*, CarMax website, 2017, accessed April 10, 2019, https://www.carmax.com/~/media/Files/cobc-10-24-17.pdf?la=en.

3. "CarMax Social Responsibility," accessed April 10, 2019, https://social -responsibility.carmax.com/.

4. "Carmax Social Responsibility – Our Environment," accessed April 10, 2019, https://socialresponsibility.carmax.com/.

5. Michael E. Porter and Mark R. Kramer, "Creating Shared Value," *Harvard Business Review* 89 nos. 1/2 (2011): 62–77.

6. "SC Johnson: Our Company," accessed April 9, 2019, http://www .scjohnson.com/en/a-family-company.

7. "SC Johnson: Our Sustainability Reports," accessed April 9, 2019, http:// www.scjohnson.com/en/our-purpose/sustainability-report.

8. *SC Johnson 2017 Sustainability Report*, SC Johnson & Son Inc., 2018, accessed April 9, 2019, https://corp-uc1.azureedge.net/-/media/sc-johnson /our-purpose/sustainability-reports/2017/scjohnson2017sustainability report.pdf.

9. "This We Believe: Our Company Values Have Guided SC Johnson for Five Generations," accessed April 9, 2019, https://www.scjohnson .com/en/a-family-company/what-it-means-to-be-a-family-company /this-we-believe-our-company-values-have-guided-sc-johnson-for-five -generations.

10. Sybille Sachs and Edwin Ruhli, *Stakeholders Matter: A New Paradigm for Strategy in Society* (Cambridge: Cambridge University Press, 2013).

11. "American Express | Our Mission Is Helping Others Accomplish Theirs," accessed April 15, 2019, https://about.americanexpress.com/our -strategy-and-mission.

12. "American Express | We Back Our Colleagues So They Can Back Their Communities," accessed April 15, 2019, https://about.americanexpress .com/we-engage-our-colleagues.

13. "American Express | Backing the People Who Are Moving the World Forward," accessed April 15, 2019, https://about.americanexpress.com /we-develop-leaders.

14. "About 3M | 3M United States," accessed April 9, 2019, https://www.3m .com/3M/en_US/company-us/about-3m/.

15. "3M Sustainability – 3M United States," accessed April 9, 2019, https:// www.3m.com/3M/en_US/sustainability-us/.

16. *3Mgives Annual Report 2017*, 3M, 2017, accessed April 9, 2019, https:// multimedia.3m.com/mws/media/1527766O/3mgives-annual-report -2017.pdf.

17. "Ethics & Compliance | Ethics & Compliance | 3M United States," accessed April 9, 2019, https://www.3m.com/3M/en_US/ethics-compliance/.

18. "3M's Commitment to Ethics & Compliance," accessed April 9, 2019, https://www.3m.com/3M/en_US/ethics-compliance/our-commitment/.

19. *ESG Report 2018* (Alibaba Group Holding Limited, 2018). Accessed April 12, 2019, https://esg.alibabagroup.com/ui/pdfs/Alibaba-ESG -Report-2018-Letter-from-the-Chairman.pdf.

20. Abigail Beall, "In China, Alibaba's Data-Hungry AI Is Controlling (and Watching) Cities," *Wired UK*, May 30, 2018, last modified September 12, 2019, https://www.wired.co.uk/article/alibaba-city-brain-artificial -intelligence-china-kuala-lumpur.

21. Brian Uzzi, "Social Structure and Competition in Interfirm Networks: The Paradox of Embeddedness," *Administrative Science Quarterly* 42 no. 1 (1997): 35–67.

22. Dejun Tony Kong, Kurt T. Dirks, and Donald L. Ferrin, "Interpersonal Trust Within Negotiations: Meta-Analytic Evidence, Critical Contingencies, and Directions for Future Research," *Academy of Management Journal* 57 no. 5 (2014): 1235–55.

23. Celia Moore, James R. Detert, Linda Klebe Treviño, Vicki L. Baker, and David M. Mayer, "Why Employees Do Bad Things: Moral Disengagement and Unethical Organizational Behavior," *Personnel Psychology* 65: 1–48.

8. REALIZING THE NEW STORY

1. The New York Life story is based on conversations with New York Life executives, as well as published sources.

2. "Our Social Impact," *New York Life*, accessed September 12, 2019, https://www.newyorklife.com/who-we-are/our-social-impact.

3. There are a number of resources for rediscovering purpose. Of particular note are: Raj Sisodia, Timothy Henry, and Thomas Eckschmidt, *Conscious Capitalism Field Guide* (Boston: Harvard Business Review Press, 2018); and Jeanne Liedtka, Tim Ogilvie, and Rachel Brozenske, *Designing for Growth: A Design Thinking Toolkit for Managers* (New York: Columbia University Press, 2011).

4. "Profit Through Purpose," *Unilever*, accessed September 12, 2019, https://www.unileverusa.com/news/news-and-features/2019/profit-through-purpose-eight-years-of-pioneering-and-learning.html.

5. "About Our Strategy," *Unilever*, accessed May 19, 2019, https://www.unilever.com/sustainable-living/our-strategy/about-our-strategy/and "Overview," accessed May 19, 2019, https://www.unilever.com/sustainable-living/overview/; and James Murray, "How Unilever Integrates the SDGs Into Corporate Strategy," *GreenBiz*, October 15, 2018, last modified September 12, 2019, https://www.greenbiz.com/article/how-unilever-integrates-sdgs-corporate-strategy.

6. "The Hershey Company: Shared Goodness," accessed April 17, 2019, https://www.thehersheycompany.com/en_us/shared-goodness.html.

7. "DonationXchange," accessed April 17, 2019, https://www.donationx.org/eDonorQuiz.aspx?s=1752f3f7-2a77-44a6-811b-b85ec6d93d17.

8. "Cocoa Sustainability," accessed April 17, 2019, https://www.thehershey-company.com/en_ca/responsibility/good-business/creating-goodness/cocoa-sustainability.html.

9. "How Major Companies Motivate Their Employees," *Next Generation* blog, accessed September 12, 2019, https://www.nextgeneration.ie/how-major-companies-motivate-their-employees/.

10. Information on The Container Store comes from extensive interviews and conversations with Kip Tindell and other employees and stakeholders.

11. "What We Stand For | The Container Store," accessed April 1, 2019, http://standfor.containerstore.com/.

INDEX

Page numbers in *italics* indicate figures or tables.